Fiction Gift A...

C000263808

SKIN

A BIOGRAPHY

SKIN
A BIOGRAPHY

SHARAD P. PAUL

FOURTH ESTATE • *New Delhi*

First published in India in 2013 by Fourth Estate
An imprint of HarperCollins *Publishers*

Copyright © Dr Sharad P. Paul 2013

ISBN: 978-93-5029-403-1

2 4 6 8 10 9 7 5 3 1

Dr Sharad P. Paul asserts the moral right to be identified
as the author of this book.

The views and opinions expressed in this book are the author's
own and the facts are as reported by him, and the publishers are
not in any way liable for the same.

Though every effort has been made to trace copyright holders and seek
permission for text quoted, it has not been possible to do so in a few cases,
where either the copyight holder could not be traced or did not respond to
repeated requests. Any omission brought to our notice will be acknowledged
in future editions.

All rights reserved. No part of this publication may be reproduced,
stored in a retrieval system, or transmitted, in any form or by any
means, electronic, mechanical, photocopying, recording or otherwise,
without the prior permission of the publishers.

HarperCollins *Publishers*
A-53, Sector 57, NOIDA, Uttar Pradesh – 201301, India
77-85 Fulham Palace Road, London W6 8JB, United Kingdom
Hazelton Lanes, 55 Avenue Road, Suite 2900, Toronto, Ontario M5R 3L2
and 1995 Markham Road, Scarborough, Ontario M1B 5M8, Canada
25 Ryde Road, Pymble, Sydney, NSW 2073, Australia
31 View Road, Glenfield, Auckland 10, New Zealand
10 East 53rd Street, New York NY 10022, USA

Typeset in 11/14 Dante MT
Jojy Philip New Delhi 110 015

Printed and bound at
Thomson Press (India) Ltd.

For Natasha, my daughter

To my parents, Samadhanam and Lily—for teaching me that
medicine is not about treating illness but human beings

Contents

Acknowledgements

I dedicate this book to my late uncle Dr Arthur S. Thambiah, a dermatologist of international renown. Uncle Bobby, as I knew him, established the Department of Dermatology at Madras Medical College and Government General Hospital, Chennai. The dermatology department, the first clinical sub-speciality to be set up at the Madras Medical College, was founded by Lt Col. J.M. Skinner of the Indian Medical Services, in what was then British India. My uncle, a decorated officer in the Indian Army, succeeded Skinner. In 1961, the first professorial chair was instituted, and Dr Thambiah was made the first professor of dermatology. He quickly developed an international reputation as one of India's foremost dermatologists. He modelled the Department of Dermatology after the Institute of Dermatology at St John's Hospital, London, and to his clinical dermatology division he added a dermatopathology service, a mycology wing and a contact dermatitis clinic.

Uncle Bobby lived his life *for* dermatology. He kept up his practice until his death at the age of eighty-seven, and was keenly interested in my career in plastic surgery, especially my burgeoning interest in skin cancer and reconstructive surgery. We spent long hours discussing the many nuances of skin and cutaneous diseases.

He didn't have a television or a wife, but he needed neither. His time was filled with diagnosing skin problems and several million grateful patients; the rest was spent in conversations with God. I remember the legendary queues outside his house at 5.30 a.m. when the first patients would try to get in. While he charged no fees for students, widows, policemen or servicemen, he treated young and old, the wealthy and the wounded, the politician and the pauper alike. When Madras University celebrated its centenary, he was the only professor to be awarded the DSc as an honour. He did not live to see this book completed. *Fare thee well*, Uncle Bobby. May you rest in peace.

Foreword

Many people, other than the author, contribute to the making of a book, from the first person who had the bright idea of alphabetic writing through the inventor of moveable type to the lumberjacks who felled the trees that were pulped for its printing. It is not customary to acknowledge the trees themselves, though their commitment is total.
– Forsyth and Rada in *Machine Learning*[1]

Writing this biography of skin was a journey—a meandering path that took me down lanes of evolution, anthropology, genetics and biochemistry. My first medical residency training was in plastic surgery, and my medical practice and research are mainly in the fields of cutaneous surgery and cutaneous oncology. While I have researched widely over the years, my technical expertise is in the fields of skin cancer and surgery. I am not an expert on genetics, biochemistry or evolution—more a jack of those sciences and a master of none—therefore I hope *real* experts will allow me some latitude for my somewhat liberal interpretations.

This book is for people like me: intellectually curious and intent on expanding already existing knowledge, while trying to make sense of the mystery of evolution. I hope it will trigger my readers' curiosity, and lead them to bigger and better voyages of their own. This is also why *Skin: A Biography* is not an exhaustive, one-stop resource, like a textbook would be.

In the course of my own research over the past 20 years, and over the past decade as a researcher and senior lecturer in skin cancer at the University of Queensland, Australia, I have developed a keen interest in the comparative biology of the different skin types.

Understanding the evolution of skin and the origin of skin colour— in essence, the adaptation of this organ to specific geographical environments—is critical to developing skin treatments. In January 2012, I presented some of my research into bio-engineering cosmetics for brown and Asian skin at the Hong Kong International Forum in Plastic Surgery and Cosmetic Medicine. This research further reiterated what I have come to realize: each skin type has unique characteristics; one treatment does not fit all.

But first, what of skin itself? When was this magnificent organ born? The story goes back to a flat and primeval earth, where the sun was dominant and the seas shallow. Fossils buried and unearthed, unicellular and multicellular, all told this evolutionary tale of the development of skin into an organ, and the changes it undertook every time the future of a species was at stake. Many of these changes were facilitated by the *same* genes observed in primitive creatures. These genes seem to possess a secret genealogical memory, a subliminal understanding of the architectural plans for our largest organ—to make it capable of both ordinary touch and rich communication with the outside world.

Many organs developed ambitiously and then failed the 'evolutionary test' to end up as vestigial appendages. Unlike *skin*, which remains smugly secure in the knowledge that evolution and adaptation are symbiotically indispensable to each other.

Dr Sharad P. Paul
www.sharadpaul.com

Note

1.   Richard Forsyth, R. Rada, *Machine Learning: Applications in Expert Systems & Information Retrieval*, Ellis Horwood Ltd, 1986.

ONE

Simply Wanting to Exist

> Human skin is porous; the world flows through you. Your
> senses are large pores that let the world in. By being attuned
> to the wisdom of your senses, you will never become an
> exile in your own life, an outsider lost in an external spiritual
> place that your will and intellect have constructed.
> – John O'Donohue, *Anam Cara: A Book of Celtic Wisdom*[1]

I'm not even sure if the birth of skin qualifies as a legitimate birth. It was more the gradual evolution of something extraordinary—over millions of years, an omnipresent organ came into being. As time went by, it took on more and more complex functions. Different genes made cameos appearances in its story, like mushrooms or toadstools on clammy clay, creating many new appendages and waxen protrusions. But many of these apparitions had roots in the ancient past, indicative of some grand unseen design scheme. Take, for example, a starfish: a heartless, brainless creature that loves to shuck oysters (or should that be *heartlessly* shucks oysters). Guess what? It has a well-developed spiny skin layer (which, by the way, makes it an 'echinoderm'). Right through evolution, it was clear that skin simply *wanted* to exist. And in the end, our body ended up getting what it asked for.

The story of skin is one of the most complex, sweeping tales of evolution. Any scientist contemplating this journey will have to make some choices, such as what bits to tell, which ones to leave out. I hope readers will feel that this excursion of mine captures something of the history and life of skin—an organ that is for me both a vocation and a passion.

This book started with a bit of monkey business.

I run a busy skin cancer surgical practice, and teach skin cancer surgery at the universities of Queensland, Australia, and Auckland, New Zealand. Since my research covers various aspects of skin, sun damage, wound care and skin care, I am often called upon to offer advice to different specialities within medicine or to other groups. Like I said earlier, my particular interests are the comparative biology of skin and the evolution of skin. My academic interests aside, no other organ excites, irritates and also envelopes our very being like skin does. When Martin Luther King Jr made his famous civil rights speech, 'I Have a Dream', it was all about binding closer a nation deeply divided by perceptions of skin colour. Nearly five decades later, I am astounded to find that most matrimonial advertisements in Indian newspapers still seek 'fair' grooms or brides (should they not be seeking fairness of character rather than skin?); I had hoped that things would have changed in the two decades that I had lived outside India. Perhaps an understanding of the history of skin—and, indeed, skin colour—will allow people to examine their attitude towards it and the fatuousness of prejudice based on skin colour.

But to return to my story, Craig Pritchard, director of Veterinary Services at the Auckland Zoo and manager, New Zealand Centre for Conservation Medicine, sometimes asks me for advice with skin problems in animals, or if an animal needs reconstructive surgery. (I often joke that in the Western world animals are more prized than humans. For example, when I have to operate on a skin cancer patient, and try to get one of my nurses to assist me on a weekend, it is often a difficult task. But if I said I was operating on a tiger on a Sunday, I would have to select from a long list of applicants clamouring to assist me.)

A few months ago, Craig rang me about an orang-utan called Melur (*see plate section*). The poor ape had dry skin on her palms, and it was peeling and cracking. When I went to examine Melur, I was warned that she'd have an offspring sitting on her shoulders that was likely to spit on me. 'Don't react,' I was advised. 'That only encourages them.'

Melur's palms were crusty and scabby; I thought she had a condition called 'dermatophilus'. This condition is caused by an actinomycete bacterium, a gram-positive bacterium that also behaves like a fungus. (Gram stain, named after Hans Christian Gram, is a method of staining that detects peptidoglycans, which are abundant in the cell walls of 'gram-positive' bacteria. This is almost always the first step in classifying bacteria in microbiological laboratory analyses.)

Actinomycetes are rather confused beings, biologically speaking: they are like unicellular bacteria, but do not contain cell walls typical of other bacteria. Further, their 'cell wall' contains neither chitin (which is found in other fungal cell walls) nor cellulose (found in plant cell walls). However, actinomycetes do produce hyphae, which are branching filamentous structures that are characteristic of fungi (*see Figure 1*).

These hyphae break off to form spores, which is a reproductive mechanism similar to pollination in plants. Melur's suspected condition, dermatophilus, is therefore a bacterial wolf in fungal clothing. It afflicts animals and sometimes humans, and is often referred to as 'mud fever' or 'rain scald'. Given Auckland's rainy, wet, temperate climate and the presence of scabs and crusts, I diagnosed Melur's condition as dermatophilus. We decided to get some biopsies of her skin when she was due for her annual check-up (which by the way, didn't show dermatophilus). During the procedure, I had to part her orange hair and sample the black-crusted skin beneath.

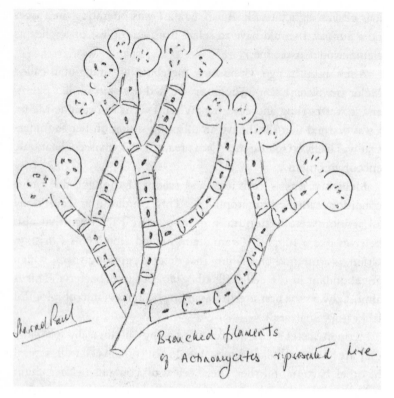

Branched filaments of Actinomycetes represented here

FIGURE 1   **Actinomycetes**

One of the trick questions kids like asking is: what colour is the skin of a polar bear? (Answer: black.) Most apes have pink skin; orang-utans, being an exclusively Asian species, mostly have brown skin under brownish or orange fur.

One of the great evolutionary questions to do with skin is this: why do apes in Africa have pink skin, while polar bears have black skin? Black skin helps polar bears retain body heat from the sun, while preventing skin from burning. While dark skin does not absorb Vitamin D due to the melanin deposits, polar bears have a diet rich in vitamins A and D, sourced from salmon and other fish. If you think about it, Arctic folk like Inuit are dark-skinned too, as they are virtually human polar bears.

So how did skin and different skin colours first evolve, and what makes skin unique? When was skin 'born'?

The very basic point of uniqueness is that while all other organs are localized to specific sites in or on our bodies, skin envelopes our entire body, making it the largest organ in the human body. This enveloping effect creates a porous partition, both separating us from and connecting us to the outside world.

Joanna Robinson's portrayal of skin in her essay 'Skin Deep'[2] is one of the most elegant I've read:

> Of all borders none feels as fundamental as our skin. Bounded by skin, we are defined territories, portable countries. The solid, soft and liquid of us are contained and identified; we do not spill, drop parts of ourselves here and there, or mix up our being with other substances in the world. Skin makes us separate and sovereign.

There is a saying that even walls need openings for dreams to escape. Skin understands this. The porous nature of this 2mm-thick wall of separation ensures that our bodies are always 'open' and ready to receive 'messages' from the environment.

The area of human skin is estimated to be around 1.8m², a measurement first arrived at by Dubois and Dubois in 1915.

$$A_{Dubois} = 0.202 \, M^{0.425} \, L^{0.725} \, m^2$$

If we wish to calculate our skin surface area, this equation is one we can use. M is our weight in kilograms and L is our height in metres. The range in skin surface area from school kids to adults is between 0.8 and 2.4 sq. m.

Let's do some ball-parking here: The average area of skin is 1.8m². If you took an area of skin that measures 6cm² it would contain around 20 blood vessels, 600 sweat glands and 60,000 melanocytes (melanin-containing cells). These melanocytes, which are cells in the basal or bottom layer of the epidermis (epidermis is the outer layer of skin, while dermis is the deeper layer), produce melanin: the pigment that determines our skin colour. Remarkably, it is the level of this *single* chemically inert and stable visual pigment that is responsible for producing *all* shades of skin colours known to mankind. These melanin-containing cells (melanocytes) are interesting to observe under a microscope; they are dendritic, with many sharp spike-like tentacles. These spikes are used like syringes—cells that inject melanin deposits, or melanosomes, into keratinocytes (I'll come to this soon) to give skin its colour. Each melanocyte supplies melanosomes to about 36 keratinocytes.

While skin colour varies between races among humans, the density of melanocytes in a given area is the same, no matter which race a person is from. So, if we were to measure the number of melanocytes per cm^2 in the arm, all humans would have around 10,000 melanocytes.

The epidermis is inherently 'dead', as it gets no direct blood supply. Cells in the epidermis generally have origins in the basal layer, and as they divide, they migrate upwards, towards the outside surface of the skin. As this movement takes place, they are filled with a dry protein called keratin, which is what makes up both hair and nails. These keratin-filled cells are called keratinocytes. Basically, the process is like sun-drying a mango, Indian-style, for pickling (or sun-drying tomatoes in Italy). As it dries, the pulp becomes dehydrated, thicker and harder. During the stage that keratin is formed, an oily lipid-complex (composed of layers of fatty acids) is formed, which spreads between cells to form a barrier layer.

Melanocytes are located in the basal layer of the epidermis, and each melanocyte is related (functionally speaking) to keratinocytes in the epidermis and fibroblasts in the dermis. (In medical nomenclature, 'blasts' are active cells that build tissue, 'clasts' destroy tissue and the in-between relatively inactive 'cytes' are the mature forms that are involved in day-to-day metabolism. (So, for instance, a fibroblast is a cell that builds connective tissue and collagen, while fibrocytes circulate in the blood stream. Blasts and cytes are essentially similar cells in different states of activity.)

Around one-tenth of the basal layer's keratinocytes produce melanin and are therefore called epidermal melanocytes. Each of these cells in turn supplies just under 40 supra-basal keratinocytes, i.e., keratinocytes that have migrated to the outer epidermal layer. The production of melanin and migration of keratinocytes (with their melanin) to the outer layers create a barrier against the environment, especially against ultraviolet (UV) damage from the sun's rays.

The constant migration of keratinocytes from the basal layer of the epidermis upwards makes them appear like a thread between the epidermis and dermis.

If I were to imagine the life of those little keratinocytes, it would be like this: the feeling of ascending a climbing rope. Perhaps they fear that if they stop moving, they would simply accumulate in one place, lumpier and lumpier, and the rope of skin would be weighed low, or would split down the middle. We'll never know if this is a rational fear, because they never stop—like serial trespassers or migrants, keratinocytes are never satisfied.

It used to be thought that brown-skinned individuals had more melanocytes. Today we know this is not true. The number of melanocytes is the same across ethnic groups, but the sizes of melanosomes, the pigment they deposit, do vary. The darker you are, the larger the melanosome. In brown skin, a single large melanosome fills each cell, rather like a ball, whereas in white skin, there are many tiny melanosomes in each cell, like small dots. The large single melanosome in brown skin absorbs more light, causing the skin to grow darker when exposed to sun.

Many people don't realize that brown skin tans more easily than white skin. Very fair skin, like in people with red or fair blonde hair, freckles rather than tans, because the melanosomes in their skin cells are tiny and multiple and cannot create an evenly tanned skin tone. I often joke with my students that freckling is just a pathetic attempt at tanning.

Tanning is also a defence mechanism that prevents our brown skin from developing severe sun damage, which can lead to skin cancer. It is frightening that melanin, the tiny dots of black that happily inhabit us, also sometimes cruelly infiltrate us to cause an extremely aggressive form of skin cancer: malignant melanoma.

Now that we've established that our skin pigmentation is largely due to differing melanin levels, we are forced to think about not just what life once was in a different time and place—when the entire human race had the same skin colour—but also the language of colour that maps our world and emotions.

When I was travelling through India for the launch of my novel, To Kill a Snow Dragonfly,[3] I couldn't help thinking about the generous amounts of sunshine and air pollution. Air pollution, while it depletes the ozone layer of the atmosphere, paradoxically reduces the amount of ultraviolet radiation that reaches ground level—the air pollutants act as a filter. Studies have shown that the more air pollution there is, the less UV radiation makes it through.[4] If India were to tap into solar energy, it would produce more solar energy than the country could consume. In a review of energy resources,[5] it was reported that the daily average solar energy incidence over India varies from 4 to 7 kWh/m^2, with about 1,500–2,000 sunshine hours per year (depending upon location). The energy yield from tapping into this would be far more than the country's current total energy consumption. For example, even assuming a solar energy production efficiency as low as 10 per cent, the output would still be a thousand times greater than the domestic electricity demand projected for 2015.

The ozone layer filters out about 97 per cent of the UV rays. When it was discovered in the early 1970s that the ozone layer had developed a large hole over Australasia and Antarctica, CFCs (chloro-fluorocarbon) were banned from aerosol sprays and refrigerants in many developed countries. The effect of this has been to greatly reduce the ozone hole, now only 25 per cent of what it was thirty years ago. This is one of the great triumphs of environmental public health measures. Still, as the earth has a tilt and the sun's rays slant into the lower reaches of the southern hemisphere, Australia and New Zealand have some of the highest UV levels in the world. Clean, relatively unpolluted air and plenty of sunshine Down Under also make for very high UV radiation levels.

It would be easier to understand the earth's tilt, and the radiation (both visible and ultraviolet) it is exposed to from the sun, if we imagine a top spinning at a tilt while orbiting an illuminated ball. If you shone a torch at night straight down at the ground, you'd get a smaller circle of light than if you held it at an incline. When held at an angle, the light falls over a wider, more oval area—which explains why the poles end up getting more radiation. And so, at different times, the north and the south poles selectively receive more light, simply because a top that spins at a tilt tends to wobble. However, the southern hemisphere regions are more vulnerable because the ozone layer over it fluctuates and thins out more easily. Why is there greater ozone depletion at the southern hemisphere? This is because the north and south poles have different characteristics: Antarctica is a snowy mountain, while the Arctic is essentially ice floating on water. Snow reflects 20 to 100 per cent of all wavelengths (depending on how 'pure' it is), whereas water only reflects 6 to 12 per cent of visible light (and half that amount of UVB radiation). At sea level, there is virtually no UVC radiation as the atmosphere absorbs most of it.

Of course, this is an overly simplistic explanation of the ozone 'hole'. Ozone is O_3, which is produced when the oxygen (O_2) in the atmosphere absorbs UVC radiation (*see Table 1 below*). Therefore, this ozone layer fluctuates with the sunspot cycle as well as with the season. It is, for instance, especially deficient in the Antarctic spring, after a long summer.

I've listed the main types of UV radiation below, based on wavelengths, and compared them to visible light and microwaves.

TABLE 1   Wavelengths of different types of radiation

Radiation source	Frequencies
X-Ray	0.1–100 angstroms
Vacuum	10–200 nanometres
Ultraviolet C (UVC)	200–290 nanometres
Ultraviolet B (UVB)	290–320 nanometres
Ultraviolet A (UVA)	320–400 nanometres
Visible light	400–700 nanometres
Near infrared	0.74–1.5 micrometres
Middle infrared	1.5–5.6 micrometres
Far infrared	5.6–1,000 micrometres
Microwave/Radio waves	greater than one millimetre

While about 97 per cent of UV rays are filtered out, the 3 per cent that reaches the earth's surface is made up of both UVA and UVB radiation. In general, UVA radiation can penetrate through transparent clothing or glass, and most sunscreen lotions (except those with specific UVA screens) do not protect against UVA radiation. UVA rays have been implicated in causing melanomas, the deadliest form of skin cancer.

UVB radiation generally causes sunburn in fair skin and tanning in brown skin types. It may sometimes cause the skin to peel, another sign of skin damage. Peeling is the result of the body killing its own cells in an attempt to repair the damage to the outer layer—a sort of kamikaze defence. Scientists call this 'apoptosis', which sounds suitably dire. UVB rays are the ones usually implicated in skin cancers, especially the more common non-melanoma skin cancers, like squamous cell cancers. ('Squamous' means 'scale-like'; squamous cell cancers therefore arise in surface tissues that shed 'squames' or scales constantly, like skin or lips. These are located above the basal layer of the epidermis. Basal cell cancers, the commonest skin cancer, arise in the basal layer of the epidermis.)

Let's step back and look at the *ABC of UV radiation*:

Ultraviolet A: ageing (causes wrinkling of skin; implicated in melanoma skin cancers in white skin; penetrates the dermis)

Ultraviolet B: burning (causes sunburn in white skin, and tanning in Indian and brown skin types; penetrates epidermis; implicated in non-melanoma skin cancers)

Ultraviolet C: cataracts (fortunately, most UVC is filtered out by the atmosphere, but looking directly at the sun is harmful; these wavelengths are especially harmful to the eyes in the Antarctic spring)

One of the great things about science is that it is littered with missing links just waiting to be discovered. Remember the puzzles where you join numbered dots to eventually create the shape of an animal or object? In the study of comparative biology and evolution, new findings could have a few missing dashes. But when most of the dots have been connected, we tend to then use the 'laws of probability' and create an image that we can assume is correct. And so it is that the theory of ultraviolet radiation being *the* cause of skin cancer cannot be proven beyond doubt, even though it is likely.

Australia's Great Barrier Reef lies directly under the 'ozone hole' we discussed and, therefore, even fish, like coral trout, in that region have been found to develop dark patches of melanoma skin cancers on their bodies (we don't know if that makes them less tasty or harmful to eat). And as UV radiation can penetrate water up to 60 metres, it is the likely culprit.

On the other hand, infrared radiation makes up half of solar radiation, while ultraviolet rays make up less than a tenth. These infrared rays generate free radicals and age skin. But do they have a greater role in skin cancer production than ultraviolet rays? Is this why sunscreens haven't had a significant impact in reducing skin cancer rates? Time will reveal new facts that will further our understanding. To quote Winston Churchill, even if out of context, 'Only one link of the chain of destiny can be handled at a time.'[6]

Figure 2 puts the different wavelengths, from the small gamma rays to the large radio waves in perspective, by comparing their sizes to familiar objects.[7]

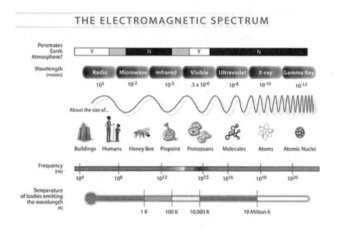

FIGURE 2   The electromagnetic spectrum

The 'UV index' was developed in 1992 by scientists from Environment Canada. Later, the World Health Organization adopted a standardized Ultraviolet Index. This UV index is a measure of the intensity of ultraviolet rays that reach the Earth's surface at a given point and many countries broadcast this measure daily as part of weather reports. Canada was the first to measure and report the daily UV indices.

This computerized model calculates ozone levels (thickness of ozone layer) and relates it to UV incidence, i.e., the incoming UV radiation level on the ground. It takes into account cloud cover (by factoring in a CMF or cloud modifying factor) and also the elevation of cities. We end up with a numerical representation of the UV index on a scale. This is the figure that weather reports cite to help people plan their degree of sun exposure on a given day.

When the UV index was first developed on a scale from 0 to 11, nobody realized that the highest UV levels due to factors like location, clear skies and ozone depletion would be close to the South Pole. Carnarvon in western Australia has recorded a UV index of 17, and New Zealand sees a UV index of 12 in peak summer. The UV index in Delhi in summer is around 10. The UV index is maximal between the hours of noon and 4 p.m., and it is generally best to avoid going out in the sun during those hours *anywhere* in the world. Exposure during peak sun hours increases tanning as well as the risk of sunburn (and degrees of both vary in different skin types).

How does knowing the UV index help us plan our sun exposure? This is where an understanding of our Fitzpatrick Skin Type helps.

Thomas B. Fitzpatrick was professor of dermatology at Harvard for nearly 40 years, after having been recruited from the University of Oregon in 1958 at the age of 39 to become the youngest professor at Harvard. He loved to quote Oliver Wendell Holmes: 'Historic continuity with the past is not a duty, it is only a necessity.' He may as well have been talking about the genetic evolution of skin.

In 1972, Thomas Fitzpatrick embarked on a study of the skin's response to UV radiation from the sun in Brisbane, Australia. Brisbane, where I teach at the University of Queensland, is Australia's 'sunshine state' (as car number plates issued by the government in Queensland proclaim with kitschy pride), with the world's highest incidence of skin cancers. Fitzpatrick learnt from the results of this Brisbane study to classify skin responses of fair-skinned Australians who participated in his study of midday sun exposure (most participants in this study were *paid* volunteers recruited from a local hospital). Interestingly, he first came up with the idea for this study to understand what would make for safe doses of UV radiation, as UVA treatment was being increasingly used in the treatment of skin diseases like psoriasis.

Fitzpatrick's research in Brisbane was limited to white Australians' skin, which he classified as skin types I to IV. Nowadays, most dermatologists or plastic surgeons interpret the Fitzpatrick skin types to mean:

❖ Type I: Always burns, never tans (like the typical Irish redhead or platinum blonde)

❖ Type II: Burns easily, tans with difficulty (usually blonde and blue-eyed)

❖ Type III: Rarely burns, tans easily (usually brown-black-haired and brown-eyed)

❖ Type IV: Sometimes burns, tans easily (Mediterranean, Spanish or lighter Indian skin)

❖ Type V: Dark brown skin that never burns, but tans easily (darker Indian skin, some North African skin)

❖ Type VI: Black African skin (skin that has abundant melanin and does not burn, but tans easily, although this darkening is often not visible due to the extremely dark skin tone)

From a practical point of view, knowing your Fitzpatrick skin type and the UV index we discussed earlier is very useful if you are trying to calculate safe sun exposure. Table 2 shows estimated 'burn times' for various skin types when exposed to the sun.

TABLE 2   **'Burn time' of different skin types**

Skin type 1 Maximum time in the sun = 67 minutes / UV index	**Skin type 2** Maximum time in the sun = 100 minutes / UV index
Skin type 3 Maximum time in the sun = 200 minutes / UV index	**Skin type 4** Maximum time in the sun = 300 minutes / UV index

Using the *modified* Fitzpatrick chart above, we know that Type 4 Indian skin can have safe sun exposure of 300 minutes/

UV index. As the UV index of Delhi is typically 10 in summer, safe sun exposure would be only about 30 minutes. If one uses a sunscreen of spf 15 (spf stands for 'sun-protection factor'), the safe sun-exposure limit is multiplied by 15 (in this example, 30*15 = 450 minutes), provided the sunscreen is reapplied every few hours. For someone with Type 1 Celtic skin living in New Zealand, where the UV index can get up to 12, the maximum time in the sun (without burning) would be 67 minutes/12, or just over five minutes. Using a sunscreen with an spf rating of 15 would increase this to around 75 minutes.

There's an interesting bit of myth-busting I'd like to do here. Unlike popular perception, an spf of 30 in your sunscreen filters out only 4 per cent more UV when compared to an spf of 15: i.e., 97 per cent versus 93 per cent. The higher the spf, the smaller the increase; an spf 50 only filters out 98 per cent of UV rays. Essentially, higher spf levels do not mean incrementally higher benefits. In fact, the US Food and Drug Administration's recent guidelines prohibit sunscreens or cosmetics from claiming a spf >50 as it gives users a false sense of security.

I tell my students that the easy way to remember this is that spf 15 lets in one in 15 harmful sunrays, while spf 30 lets in one in 30, and spf 50 lets in one in 50.

Let's not forget that *melanin* is a sunscreen. A sunscreen with an spf of 2 would allow you to double your sun exposure. Kobayashi and Nordlund, among others, studied the sun-protection factor of melanin and found that melanin has an spf of 2 to 4. In other words, it will let in one in two to one in four burning rays, and therefore absorb between 25 to 75 per cent of UV rays, usually around 50 per cent in brown skin.

To be considered an organ, a mass of tissue needs to have the functions of expiration/excretion and inspiration/absorption. In addition to being an absorptive barrier, the skin's primary functions are sensory—touch and pain—and thermoregulation. While the former makes skin a sensory organ, the human ability to sweat gives it the ability to control body temperature.

Speaking of chemistry, Carl Jung once said, 'The meeting of two personalities is like the contact of two chemical substances: if there is any reaction, both are transformed.' But what of the chemistry of skin? A quick trip down memory lane to high school chemistry class reminds us that 'pH' means 'potential of hydrogen'. I can almost hear the whiny voice of my chemistry teacher, whose name I sadly no longer recall: 'As pH is a log scale, for every unit change in pH, there is a tenfold increase or decrease in the number of hydrogen atoms present.' When pH is neutral, a substance is neither acidic or alkaline, i.e., its H+ (acidic) and OH– (alkaline) ions are balanced. Therefore, when H+ and OH– combine, we get water, which is neutral, i.e., it has a pH of 7.

The pH of human blood is regulated by the body in the range of 7.35 to 7.45. However, the pH of adult human skin is 5.5. Why the difference? When a baby is born, its pH is around 7, and this turns progressively more acidic in order to protect the tender infant skin from infections. When a child reaches puberty, due to hormonal changes, the skin is more susceptible to bacterial and fungal infections (from acne and increased sweating, etc.). In some ways, the development of bodily hair at puberty is a skin defence mechanism; as more sebaceous glands become active, it leads to more oil (sebum) production. This combination of oil and sweat decreases the pH of skin to 5.5—an acidic environment that is inherently hostile to bacteria. Some people refer to this change in skin at puberty as the development of an 'acid mantle'.

This has some practical implications. Traditional soaps are generally very alkaline, with a pH of 9–11. Using soap is therefore not ideal for skin health as it disrupts this acid mantle. This is why dermatologists usually recommend (as do I) soap-free cleansers or 'pH neutral' cleansers.

Where does the word 'skin' originate from? Etymology suggests that the word came into use c. AD 1200, and meant 'animal hide' (usually dressed or tanned).[8] The word 'skin' essentially replaced 'hide'; the modern technical distinction between these words is actually based on the size of the animal.

Leather experts distinguish rawhides thus: hides come from a large animal, e.g., a bullock or cow; skins come from smaller or young animals, e.g., calf, sheep, goat, lamb (or humans); fur comes from small animals, e.g., hares, rabbits or foxes (rawhide manuals state that this fur should be 'properly' removed by cutting at the rear legs and pulling it over the animal's head).

Nowadays the word skin is mostly used to describe the human integument, and sometimes even vegetable or fruit coverings.

Once skin was established as the largest organ in the body of humans, how did it evolve to develop different colours? Why did it need these different colours in the first place? To answer this question, we have to go back to the very beginning of time as we know it in a biological sense.

NOTES

1.   John O'Donohue, *Anam Cara: A Book of Celtic Wisdom*, HarperCollins, 1998.

2.   Joanna Robinson, 'Skin Deep', *River Teeth: A Journal of Nonfiction Narrative*, Vol. 9, No. 1, Fall 2007, pp. 36–41.

3.   First published by Fourth Estate, an imprint of HarperCollins India, January 2012.

4.   Farhad Hosseinpanah et al., 'The effects of air pollution on vitamin D status in healthy women: A cross sectional study', *BMC Public Health*, 2010; 10: 519. Published online 2010.

5.   Muneer T., Asif M., Munawwar S., 'Sustainable production of solar electricity with particular reference to the Indian economy', *Renewable & Sustainable Energy Reviews*, October 2005, 9(5), pp. 444–73.

6.   Winston Churchill, Speech in the House of Commons, 27 February

1945, quoted from 'Crimea Conference' in *The Second World War, Volume VI: Triumph and Tragedy*, Cassel & Co. Ltd, 1954.

7. 'Electromagnetic Spectrum', New World Encyclopedia, http://www.newworldencyclopedia.org/entry/Electromagnetic_spectrum?oldid=679396, accessed 17 March 2012.

8. Suggested origin from etymological dictionary Online Etymology Dictionary, http://www.etymonline.com/index.php accessed Sunday, 11 March 2012: from O.N. skinn 'animal hide', [1] from P.Gmc. *skintha- (cf. O.H.G. scinten, Ger. schinden 'to flay, skin'; Ger. dial. schind 'skin of a fruit', Flem. schinde 'bark'), [2] from PIE *sken- 'cut off' (cf. Bret. scant 'scale of a fish', Ir. scainim 'I tear, I burst'), from base *sek- 'cut'. [3] [1] O.N.: Old Norse, the Norwegian language as written and spoken c. AD 100 to 1500, the relevant phase of it being 'Viking Norse' (700–1100), the language spoken by the invaders and colonizers of northern and eastern England c. 875–950. [4] P.Gmc: Proto-Germanic, hypothetical prehistoric ancestor of all Germanic languages, including English. O.H.G: Old High German, the ancestor of the modern literary German language, spoken in the upland regions of Germany; German language as written and spoken from the earliest period to c. 1100. [5] PIE: Proto-Indo-European, the hypothetical reconstructed ancestral language of the Indo-European family. The time scale is much debated, but the most recent date proposed for it is about 5,500 years ago.

TWO

No Evolution or Destiny, Only Being

> Still there are moments when one feels free from one's own identification with human limitations and inadequacies. At such moments, one imagines that one stands on some spot of a small planet, gazing in amazement at the cold yet profoundly moving beauty of the eternal, the unfathomable: life and death flow into one, and there is neither evolution nor destiny; only being.
>
> – Albert Einstein[1]

Albert Einstein famously said that there was no evolution or destiny; only being. Charles Darwin's theory of evolution, his fierce, clear-eyed scientific determination and sheer body of work make him an emblem of what is wrong with 'creationist' theories. However, Darwin himself fluctuated between initially believing in God and more agnostic thoughts in his later years. In an 1860 letter to Harvard botanist Asa Gray, he wrote:[2]

> With respect to the theological view of the question: This is always painful to me. I am bewildered. I had no intention to write atheistically. But I own I cannot see as plainly as others do, and as I should wish to do, evidence of design and beneficence on all sides of us ...
>
> On the other hand, I cannot anyhow be contented to view this

wonderful universe, and especially the nature of man, and to conclude that everything is the result of brute force ... I grieve to say that I cannot honestly go as far as you do about Design. I am conscious that I am in an utterly hopeless muddle. I cannot think that the world, as we see it, is the result of chance; and yet I cannot look at each separate thing as the result of Design ... Again, I say I am, and shall ever remain, in a hopeless muddle.

Perhaps Darwin hedged his bets because he wondered if one day he would have to stand in front of the God of Evolution and speak of his writings that, like monstrous scientific bridges, attempt an understanding across generations of species. And the God of Evolution might have said, 'That wasn't a job all done. There are too many rivets and brackets missing—that bridge might come down any day; still needs a bit of work, son.'

But to return to our own question: how did skin become such an all-encompassing integument when organisms first moved from just a single cell to multicellular creatures? 'Oh, it wasn't a problem,' skin would say. This is actually skin's defining feature: being a free-form, loosely organized organ, it is capable of not just absorption and metabolism, but also sensation.

Sir Edmund Hillary climbed Mt Everest in 1953. Mt Everest—lofty and imposing at 8,848 metres above sea level—was considered impossible to climb. Until Edmund Hillary trampled upon that supposition. A man from one of two tiny shaky islands at the bottom of the world: a country named New Zealand, where the people are called Kiwis. Kiwis—what sort of people are named after flightless, doddery birds? Surely they must have no spark, no spirit of adventure. Maybe this motivated Hillary most of all. And do you know what he said when he finally scaled the summit, and stood on freshly fallen snow on top of the world? 'I knocked the bastard off.' No grandiose speech, no pre-written spiel and no political statement.

Speaking of snow, or snowflakes really, think about what life is like for keratinocytes, as they migrate up the epidermal layers of skin. A *constant* avalanche. Like when it has been snowing for days. *Indoors*. The momentum of snow is huge and awesome. Snowflakes keep piling up one on top of the other until they reach the ceiling; until there's not enough room and each flake begs the other one to stop pushing. The thing is, someone forgot to tell the snow that it isn't allowed indoors. So, in the end, each flake becomes flattened out. With anatomy and physiology like this, we could say that skin *is* flaky. But it is actually a beautiful process to look at under the microscope: to see cells flattening out in the outer or horny epidermal layers until they have no more room to host a nucleus.

In the same year that Hillary climbed Mt Everest, James Bond first appeared on celluloid, and the movie *Peter Pan* captured children's imaginations around the world. But 1953 was also a watershed year for science and medicine because of a few ground-breaking discoveries: on 26 March, Jonas Salk announced his polio vaccine and saved many children from a crippled life; and barely a month later, on 25 April, Francis Crick and James D. Watson published their description of the double helix structure of DNA. But in my high school science classes, a personal favourite breakthrough was the Stanley Miller experiment—which demonstrated how amino acids, the building blocks of early life, could have evolved.

In 1951, Harold Urey, a geologist from the University of Chicago, had hypothesized that Earth's primordial atmosphere would have contained water vapour, ammonia and methane, and no oxygen. At this time, Stanley Miller was a young graduate looking for someone to supervise his thesis, as his previous supervisor had left the university. He suggested to Harold Urey that he would like to simulate early Earth chemistry using Urey's theory about the composition of Earth's ancient atmosphere. In the beginning, Harold Urey was sceptical, in good part because he felt it would take too long for a graduate student to organize such an undertaking. But Stanley Miller was to prove him wrong. He set up a flask of water to represent the oceans, connected this to a flask of gases through which he passed electrical current (to represent lightning). Within two or three days, there were signs that glycine, a simple amino acid, had been created, and by the end of the week, several more of life's essential building blocks had turned up in the volatile mixture.

I can imagine Stanley Miller looking astounded at his creation of life's essential building blocks—*the story of life:* life had appeared in an instant, as if, and indeed when, struck by lightning. Stanley Miller wrote his thesis and named Harold Urey his supervisor, but Urey graciously asked him to remove his name, saying, 'I've already got my Nobel Prize.' The young and brilliant Stanley Miller had found something even rarer in the world of medicine and science: a selfless supervisor who allowed him to take full credit. Explaining that he was trying to duplicate the atmosphere prevailing in primitive Earth, rather than trying to create what would be ideal conditions for the formation of amino acids, Miller wrote:[3]

> Although in this case the total yield was small for the energy expended, it is possible that, with more efficient apparatus (such as mixing of the free radicals in a flow system, use of higher hydrocarbons from natural gas or petroleum, carbon dioxide, etc, and optimum ratios of gases), [there] would be a way of commercially producing amino acids.

Many scientists remained unbelieving. It seemed rather convenient that primitive Earth's atmosphere had such optimum conditions. It was more likely that it contained a mixture of carbon dioxide and nitrogen, which would not provide amino acids. People looked for alternative theories from outer space, like comet collisions. Stanley Miller did not have all the answers to questions about the origin of life, but he was the first to have a decent crack at explaining the origins of life's building blocks.

Nowadays everyone is familiar with the Big Bang Theory. The term was actually coined by cosmologist Fred Hoyle, even if he himself was opposed to this theory. Fred and his colleague,

Chandra Wickramasinghe, were very interested in the Miller–Urey experiments. Stanley Miller had set up his experiment to model Earth's primitive atmosphere made up of CH_4 (methane), NH_3 (ammonia), H_2 and H_2O. In 1963, Cyril Ponnamperuma and colleagues, Carl Sagan and Ruth Mariner, used high-energy electrons on a mixture similar to Miller's original formula and obtained adenine (a constituent of nucleic acids), and later ribose and deoxyribose—nucleic acids that are important components of our genetic codes. While genetic materials could be made in the lab from an artificial primordial atmosphere, most scientists were sceptical about the significance of it because the primary requirement for such synthesis was that the atmosphere needed to be reductive (chemically speaking) rather than oxidative (which is what conditions in ancient Earth were like, which we know from analyses of old rocks).

Let me pause to explain this. One of my patients, (the late) Len Castle, was one of New Zealand's best potters. Observing a potter at work is the easiest way to understand oxidative and reductive atmospheres. When a potter fires up his kiln, the increased temperature causes many substances to oxidize as long as there is oxygen available. Volatile portions of compounds and molecules break free and the remaining parts are free to attach to oxygen, forming oxides. For example, if you fired up copper carbonate in a kiln, the carbon will burn off, allowing oxygen to bond with copper to form copper oxide. This copper oxide is often used in pottery glazes to create a speckled effect.

Now let us use the potter's kiln to understand reductive atmospheres. Let's say we light a fire; it will only burn as long as oxygen is available. So if you shut the door and reduce the draft, the kiln is filled with carbon atoms that are hungry for oxygen—so hungry that they scavenge oxygen off other compounds in the clay, thereby 'reducing' the compounds contained in the clay being used. If we used the copper oxide discussed above, this is reduced to a deep red cuprite (Cu_2O). Understanding this process allows the potter to choose the colours of his products. I have a lovely pottery vase in my living room from Len Castle that has the wonderful red glaze of cuprite.

In 1969, a 'chemically primitive' meteorite slammed into Murchison, a little town in Australia. When analytical chemist Philippe Schmitt-Kopplin of the Helmholtz German Research Centre for Environmental Health in Munich and his colleagues used high-resolution mass spectrometry to look at the organic (carbon-based) content of three Murchison samples, they were astonished to find more than 14,000 unique molecular compositions, or collections of atoms, in the samples they tested. This was exciting because some scientists, like Fred Hoyle, had long held that life on Earth began with the delivery of prebiotic organic compounds from space via asteroids or comets.

Well before the Murchison meteorite, Hoyle and Wickramasinghe had proposed that if we were to take into account the planetary atmospheric clouds—which existed before planets were formed, and were caused by the explosions of stars—these had both the chemicals and high fluxes of ionizing radiation needed to produce prebiotic chemicals. They wrote:[4]

> The most promising venues for the synthesis of prebiotic molecules by Miller–Urey-type processes may be found near the centres of galaxies. Explosions of supermassive stars would produce the basic chemical elements necessary to make molecules in high-density mass flows that are then acted upon by ionizing radiation, thus simulating the conditions needed for Miller–Urey-type processing.

Charles Darwin was quoted nearly a century earlier in *The Origin of Life* by J.D. Bernal,[5] clearly thinking along the lines of Stanley Miller:

> It is often said that all the conditions for the first production of a living organism are now present, which could have ever been present. But if (and oh! what a big if!) we could conceive in some warm pond, with all sorts of ammonia and phosphoric salts, light, heat, electricity, &c., present, that a proteine compound was

chemically formed ready to undergo still more complex changes, at the present day such matter would be instantly devoured or absorbed, which would not have been the case before living creatures were formed.

Okay, so we've now generated some amino acids by heating them up in an intergalactic kiln. But heating amino acids results in polymerization, which creates polypeptides, which cannot replicate by themselves. How did these amino acids in the primordial soup reproduce to form the larger building blocks of life?

Perhaps the Nobel Prize-winning work in 1989 explained it best. Until then, it was conventional scientific wisdom that the triggering and catalysis of chemical reactions within living cells was the exclusive domain of protein molecules called enzymes. Then, in the early 1980s, biophysicist Sidney Altman of Yale University and chemist Thomas R. Cech of the University of Colorado, Boulder, found that ribonucleic acid (RNA), traditionally considered to be only a passive intracellular carrier of genetic information, can also act as an enzyme. Remember, we discussed that ribose could be synthesized from primordial atmosphere using high-energy electrons? Cech was studying the splicing of ribonucleic acid in a single-celled organism called *Tetrahymena thermophila*. He discovered, much to his surprise, that when he put an unprocessed RNA molecule into a test tube, in the absence of protein, it started to splice itself. In other words, the RNA molecule could cut itself into pieces and join the genetically important RNA fragments together again.

With the discovery of this chemically complex self-splicing reaction, in 1982, Cech's team became the first to show that RNA molecules can have both a *catalytic* and *reproductive* function. Altman and Cech concluded that this RNA is capable of catalysing a number of chemical reactions, including the polymerization of nucleotides (the basic structural units of nucleic acids). RNA is thus uniquely able to serve as both a template and a catalyst for its own replication. When the Swedish Academy awarded them the Nobel Prize, they remarked, 'Many textbooks will have to be changed.'

We know that the genes of mammalian cells have DNA and not RNA. But to understand the evolution of genetic material, we have to enter the fascinating, dramatic world of RNA, full of interesting characters.

I like using creative writing to explain scientific matters, and love the fusion between science and art—possibly because I have written two literary novels. Karen Bernardo, who is the director of the Coburn Free Library in Owego, New York, and works as a writer and editor, had this to say while discussing 'characterization in literature':[6]

> What does characterization do for a story? In a nutshell, it allows us to empathize with the protagonist and secondary characters, and thus feel that what is happening to these people in the story is vicariously happening to us; and it also gives us a sense of verisimilitude, or the semblance of living reality.

Let's examine our story and apply literary characterization.

Title: **When RNA met DNA**

Location: The cell. Essentially there are two requirements for building this set: an organism's cell needs to be able to both attach molecules and remove them; and the cell needs to be able to copy itself using both original and sometimes new architects' plans.

Characters
RNA: A rascally playboy, who continues to play the field. Age hasn't slowed him down, nor has his chronic shortage of money. We watch him, awe-struck at his daring and preoccupation with spreading his genes around. You can see him at work, linking up with both married DNA and unhitched ribosomes. He's utterly charming, ready to help the ladies with their nail polish and always quick to

top up half-empty glasses. Needless to say, viruses adore him. He is a hacker and code-breaker, and often uses messengers to carry his love notes.

From a characterization point of view, RNA is what writers would call 'dynamic'—constantly changing, resolving conflicts, facing evolutionary crises and brushing off the burden of being a central character.

The very single-stranded structure of RNA makes it mobile, flexible and light on its feet. After all, a rope can be used to scale virtually any tower as long as the climber is flexible and fit.

DNA: The stable sort. The sort of man your mother would want you to marry. Nothing too fancy—good job, nice house, good contacts, but a bit of a homebody, which is why DNA never ventures beyond his nucleus. Unfortunately, he is hopelessly addicted to computers and has a 'geekoid' personality. Works as a code-builder for the FBI; typical of the Feds to hire this kind of person. Even took an old exercise book from his son's bag. That's the only way he could think of to record his thoughts or sequences. But what you don't realize (until the end of the story) is that he was once a playboy, with a penchant for unzipping genes.

From a characterization point of view, DNA is what we'd call both 'static' and 'round': does not change much over time, but often portrayed as a conflicted or contradictory person. Remember, this is the guy who hung out with RNA and then said he didn't enjoy it. The double-stranded nature of DNA makes him stable and less risk-prone, like a wooden ladder with even rungs. While ladders are good once foundations have been laid, they are no good for navigating tight spaces, unlike a single-stranded rope.

Ribosomes: These are machining facilities, well run and well managed. They understand that the key to success and getting more business is to stick to specifications and customers' plans. These guys have lathes everywhere—turret, crankshaft, duplicating and multi-spindle lathes—you name the machine needed, and these guys are likely to have them. Their rooms may be dark and grey, but they are heavy with machinery and light on boredom.

Ribosomes are 'stock' characters, typical machinists and manufacturers with an eye for detail.

Mitochondria: The energy 'cell' or battery. Constantly tense, always on edge and with an endless appetite for physical activity. It is tiring even to look at these characters, but we need them—they are our sources of energy.

Again 'stock' characters, i.e., rather stereotypical: think chest-thumping, slogan-spouting, fitness-trainer kind of pumped-up enthusiasm.

Dicer: Interesting character and well travelled, in some ways. Started life as a *kukumete* in Kenya (that's 'cook's mate' in Kenyan household slang, I'm told). Didn't learn much more than cutting, so she should really be called a chopper. She loves to tell you she can slice, julienne, cube, dice, mince and crush ingredients, even if she prefers to julienne rather than slice (because it sounds more French and chef-like).

Editors: These are bespectacled pedants—a good example is adenosine deaminase, who insists on retyping RNA letters at various places within the mRNA or messenger RNA transcript to make sure there are no errors in the code.

Introns: These are sort of pre-fabricated pieces of wall or tile that are used as fillers whenever a piece goes missing because RNA has gifted it to a new girlfriend.

Moving on now to the rest of the set-up. Proteins are polymers of amino acids. They are manufactured by ribosomes. Proteins have many functions in cells; it is the amino acid sequence that determines the shape of a protein and what it ends up doing.

DNA stands for deoxyribose nucleic acid. Nucleotides, the individual structural units of DNA and RNA, polymerize to form nucleic acids. Nucleotides comprise a nitrogenous base, a five-carbon sugar (which may be ribose or deoxyribose) and a phosphate group (technically, if you remove the phosphate group, a nucleotide becomes a nucleoside). Nucleotides contain either a purine or a pyrimidine base (purines are adenine and guanine; pyrimidines are cytosine, uracil and thymine). Deoxyribonucleotides are nucleotides in which the sugar is deoxyribose; ribonucleotides are nucleotides in which the sugar is ribose. When nucleotides polymerize, the hydroxyl group attached to the 3' carbon of a sugar of one nucleotide forms a bond with the phosphate of another nucleotide to form a nucleic acid. RNA stands for ribose nucleic acid. Chemically speaking, a ribose sugar basically becomes deoxyribose when it loses an O_2 at 2' position, and the amino acid uracil is replaced by another pyrimidine, thymine (*see Figure 3*).

To summarize: *Proteins are polymers of amino acids, while nucleic acids are polymers of nucleotides.*

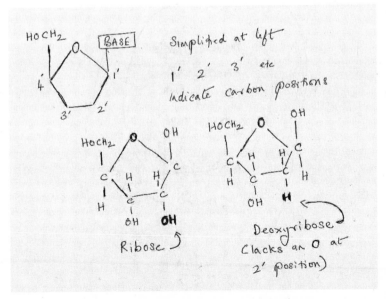

FIGURE 3   How a ribose sugar becomes deoxyribose

When we speak of hereditary characteristics, we tend to say 'it is in our DNA'. DNA stores the necessary information codes needed to build a cell. Fittingly then, it is located within a safe vault, the nucleus. DNA allows this information to be shared and reproduced when it sees fit.

A DNA code needs to be decoded by RNA to create an RNA template. As discussed earlier, the rascally RNA is both a code-breaker and hirer of messengers called mRNA. This process is what we biologically term 'transcription'. Transcription is essentially the making of an 'RNA copy' of a DNA strand (Figure 4). Therefore, this transcription process results in an RNA complement that includes uracil (U) in the places where thymine (T) would have occurred in a DNA complement.

We can divide the contents of the cell into *fats* (the lipid-rich cell membrane contains phospholipids—lipids that have a phosphate

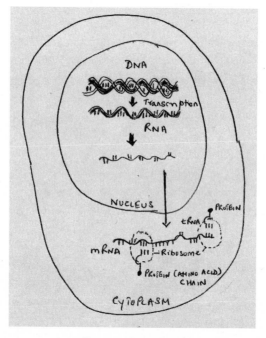

FIGURE 4   Transcription

group in their molecules, sometimes referred to as a 'fluid mosaic'), *proteins* (produced by ribosomes from nucleic acids, as seen in Figure 3, although proteins also form part of the cell membrane), *cofactors* (vitamins: many proteins require cofactors to carry out functions like scavenging or carrying O_2) and *carbohydrates* (these sugars are bound to cell membranes in the form of glycoproteins and are important in cell-to-cell recognition; that apart, they make up energy sources. Interestingly, the four human blood types designated A, B, AB and O denote 'antigens', or identifiable variations in the carbohydrate part of glycoproteins on the surface of red blood cells).

The code for ordering manufacture of a specific protein is located in the DNA; however, DNA cannot leave its nucleus—homebound, remember?—so it unzips its double spirals a little bit at the point where codes are located. This section is what we call a gene.

The mRNA mirrors this code (and therefore is initially double-stranded), and leaves the nucleus carrying instructions about manufacture given by the DNA. These are taken in secure envelopes (larger RNA pieces are sliced into smaller segments by dicer enzymes) to the factories, the ribosomes, where they become ribosomal RNA or rRNA (and during the transfer process are called transfer RNA or tRNA). (*See Figure 5.*) The instructions for manufacture are essentially sequences of three nucleotides to code for each amino acid. These sequences are called codons. Then there is also mitochondrial RNA, or mtRNA, which are located in the energy cells that power the organism.

Common sense will tell you that the chemical make-up of viruses or bacteria or starfish or humans is different. But, remarkably, their power cells are activated by the same 'energy molecules' that are located in mitochondria. The most efficient way for cells to generate energy from food or nutritional sources is through cellular respiration, which leads to production of adenosine triphosphate (ATP). Right through evolution, ATP has been essential for powering respiration in both primitive and nucleated cells.

Going back to literary characterization, let's examine the storyline.

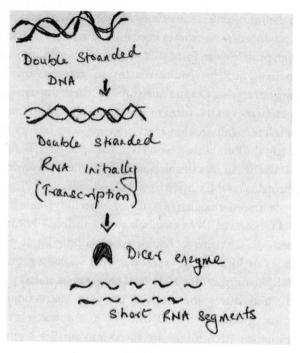

FIGURE 5   Transferring the code

Plot: Essentially this chapter looks to answer two chicken-and-egg riddles to do with genetics:

1. In all organisms, we need nucleic acids (DNA and RNA) to make new proteins; and proteins are in turn needed to create nucleic acids. So which came first: nucleic acid or protein?
2. Which came first: RNA or DNA?

Cech's experiments answered the first question—which came first, protein or nucleic acid? In demonstrating that RNA could both store genetic information and also cause chemical reactions to copy themselves, the experiments not only confirmed that nucleic acids were the first to evolve, but in a primitive world that arose out of collisions, RNA performed the functions of modern DNA (storing genetic information) and proteins (catalyzing reactions). (*See Figure 6.*)

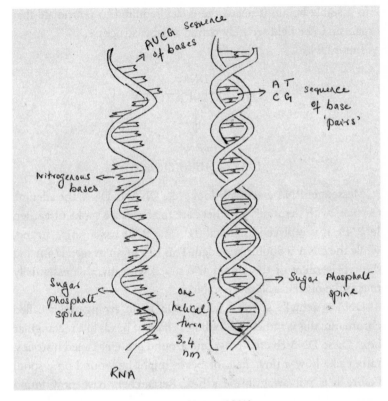

FIGURE 6   RNA and DNA

DNA (data storing) → *RNA (data reading/copying)* → *Protein (execution)*

It is obvious from Cech's studies that nucleic acids developed first, *before* protein. Primitive organisms like viruses use RNA to infect host cells. Editing a gene's mRNA by a *single* chemical letter radically alters the protein's function. Therefore, as we discussed earlier, molecular editors perform the task of making sure there are no typos in the mRNA transcript (much like my editor, Ajitha, who has pored over this manuscript, foraging for grammatical errors).

A promiscuous serially mating character is ideal for the development of new organisms, but once an animal has evolved into a stable being, it needs the codes required to reproduce that organism to be held securely within a stable structure.

Enter DNA.

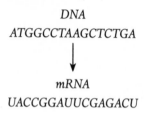

DNA
ATGGCCTAAGCTCTGA

mRNA
UACCGGAUUCGAGACU

Messenger RNA essentially looks like DNA. In DNA, the adenine (A) pairs with thymine (T)—these are the bases we spoke of earlier. In RNA, it is replaced by uracil (U). The RNA has a single strand, while the DNA is double-stranded. This loss of an oxygen atom and the replacement of the amino acid uracil with thymine essentially makes the nucleic acid more stable.

DNA is actually spooled within cells in an arrangement called chromatin; this is rather like folding a chain of beads in a rectangular box. These DNA chains are wound around proteins called histones, rather like how a tiny chain of beads might be wound on a spool before it is put away inside a box. Researchers have now found 'switches' that control access to these spools, so that the necessary DNA strand can be unfurled. C. David Allis, who works at Rockefeller University in New York, calls this the 'histone code'—a secret code that actually determines which proteins are produced, a sort of 'Da Vinci Code' for nucleic acids.

Figure 7 illustrates how DNA is stored in folded strands of chromatin, wound around spools called histones, and in chromosomes, where individual genes are located.

When researchers first set out to clone higher organisms, they found introns, stretches of DNA that did not code for any particular protein structure. Somewhat mysteriously, during transcription, all the codes, including introns, are copied into mRNA, possibly indicating a function we do not yet understand.

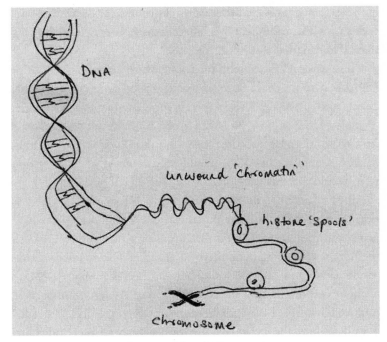

FIGURE 7   Where DNA is stored

RNA is generally believed to have been the initial genetic system, and an early stage of chemical evolution is thought to have been based on self-replicating RNA molecules—a period of evolution now scientifically known as the 'RNA World'. Such interactions between RNA and amino acids then became the modern genetic code, and DNA later replaced RNA as the genetic building block.

This evolution of DNA from RNA was recently confirmed by 'accelerated evolution' experiments. *Science Daily* reported[7] that scientists at the Scripps Research Institute had managed to convert an RNA enzyme (ribozyme) to a corresponding DNA enzyme (deoxyribozyme) through a series of chemical reactions simulating Earth's primitive atmosphere. In the beginning, the ribozyme emerged as a DNA molecule with the same RNA sequence, but with no catalytic activity (i.e., an inactive DNA version of the RNA enzyme), but as repeated cycles were carried out, the deoxyribosome ended up with the same catalytic effect as the RNA enzymes, showing that DNA essentially evolved from RNA.

This answered the second question: which came first—RNA or DNA? Maybe we could have answered this by simply studying the characters' personalities and applying some literary common sense. A stable character like DNA, with access to the secret codes, would need to be housed in a secure facility—i.e., the nucleus. On the other hand, a delinquent like RNA would need some supervision; if not, RNA would share its genetic material with all and sundry.

All of this brings us back to our own big question: why was skin born? Even unicellular organisms like choanoflagellates have genes and proteins. It is clear that organisms first developed a cell membrane to keep genetic material encased. This membrane, *like* future skin, was also phospholipid-rich and semi-permeable to facilitate communication and access nutrition. As organisms became multicellular, they essentially became a colony of cells and needed a wall around the entire colony, rather than smaller individual envelopes encasing each house. This was perhaps what led to the formation of a proper integument: *skin*.

John Burdon Sanderson Haldane was an Eton- and Oxford-educated Scotsman who went on to become one of the most influential thinkers in the field of genetics and evolutionary biology. A true polymath, with astounding scientific foresight (he even predicted test-tube babies in his writings in 1924), he was considered a bit of a rascal by the establishment (mostly for his enchantment with communist ideology). Haldane ended up migrating to India, where he found kinship in Calcutta (now Kolkata). Over 50 years ago, he was quoted as saying, somewhat prophetically:[8]

> Perhaps one is freer to be a scoundrel in India than elsewhere. So
> was one in the USA in the days of people like Jay Gould, when

(in my opinion) there was more internal freedom in the USA than there is today.

Haldane made huge contributions to the fields of genetics, biochemistry and in the study of population fitness. The dilemma for a population occurs when its genome no longer gives it an advantage in a current environment. This was how humans developed lighter skin to cope with the local sunlight-deficient conditions in Europe—when modern humans first migrated out of hot and sunny Africa, they all had black skin. (We will discuss this in more detail later in this book.) Haldane elegantly summarized our discussions in this chapter regarding evolution of organisms and their need for 'a skin' as follows: [9]

> I suggest that the primitive enzyme was a much shorter peptide of low activity and specificity, incorporating only 100 bits or so. But even this would mean one out of 1.3×10^{30} possibilities. This is an unacceptable, large number. If a new organism were tried out every minute for 10^8 years, we should need 10^{17} simultaneous trials to get the right result by chance. The earth's surface is 5×10^{18} cm^2. There just isn't, in my opinion, room. Sixty bits, or about 15 amino acids, would be more acceptable probabilistically, but less so biochemically. I suggest that the first synthetic organisms may have been something like a tobacco mosaic virus, but including the enzyme or enzymes needed for its own replication. More verifiably, I suggest that the first synthetic organisms may be so constituted. For natural, but not for laboratory life, a semipermeable membrane is needed ...

Haldane's 'bits' are a sort of 'universal probability limits' that help join the dots. As Richard Dawkins writes in his book, *The Blind Watchmaker*:[10] 'We can accept a certain amount of luck in our explanations, but not too much.'

In the battle between creation and evolution, the Biblical view of creation has been scientifically relegated to a state of acknowledged subordination. Of course, the creationist counter-argument is: if the world was created by atoms in random collisions, someone had to have an atom there in the first place. The Hindu view is in some ways a version of 'spiritual Darwinism'—a constant evolution of the spirit—that uses the organic body as the medium for many small experiments in nourishment, pleasure, mode of living, all with the aim of perfecting the body for a higher sensibility. (Every time I visit Chennai, a friend and I walk through the grounds of the Theosophical Society in Besant Nagar, named after Annie Besant, the British social reformer who had made India her home. Besant understood Eastern philosophies and viewed practices such as yoga as a way to speed up evolution, a conscious 'fast forwarding' of nature's stately processes, as opposed to Darwinian evolution, where humans are passive observers as nature potters about.)

Irrespective of beliefs in creation or evolution, everyone seems to converge on Haldane's observation: 'For natural, but not for laboratory life, a semipermeable membrane is needed.'

Enter *skin*.

BIRTH OF THE FIRST ORGAN

> Indeed, we have not any organ at all for knowings or for 'truth': we 'know' (or believe, or fancy) just as much as may be of use in the interest of the human herd, the species; and even what is here called 'usefulness' is ultimately only a belief, a fancy, and perhaps precisely the most fatal stupidity by which we shall one day be ruined.
>
> – Nietzsche in *Joyful Wisdom*[11]

The evolutionary transition from single-celled organisms to multicellular organisms has long been a mystery. Many scientists have searched for this 'missing link'. Essentially, when a cell divides, it has two options: leave 'home' and migrate to a unicellular existence or aggregate to form a multicellular organism. Interestingly, for the first 1,500 million years in the existence of eukaryotes (organisms that possess cell membranes, and cell nuclei and membrane-encased organelles, unlike single-celled prokaryotes), *not one* of the forays into multicellular states was successful, leaving the early fossil record devoid of multicellular forms. After all that time, what advantages did the unicellular creature see in becoming multicellular? If evolution is a process of natural selection, why did it take 1,500 million years for organisms to develop more than one cell?

Colonies of volvocine algae are the ideal subjects for the study of this progression, as they diverged from being unicellular to multicellular forms relatively recently (from an evolutionary point of view, a mere 35 million years ago), and therefore provide a unique window of opportunity to study evolution in progress. In other multicellular creatures, the factors that determined their history lie buried under hundreds of millions of years of biological contemplation.

Volvocine algae are photosynthetic organisms that range from unicellular forms, like chlamydomonas, to complete multicellular forms, like volvox, which have 500 to 50,000 cells and exhibit germ–somatic cell separation (cells separated into having metabolic/structural [somatic] and reproductive [germ] functions, which we term germ–soma separation). These volvocine algae fossils also exhibit in-between forms without germ–somatic cell separation, like gonium, where each cell gives rise to a daughter colony, but dies after reproduction. Given this relatively short evolutionary period, we are able to study the genetics of the whole gamut of changes: from single cell, to single cell without germ–soma separation, to multicellular forms with fully separated germ–soma cells. The genes necessary for group-living and 'social reorganization' of these colonies were identified in the algae *Volvox carteri* in 1999.

For a start, increasing group size consumes more local resources, exactly as it would if we were planning a new colony in a city. Also, moving to a multicellular state limited the motility of these volvocine algae. These creatures have flagella to assist their motion, but these are located on one side of a cell. Therefore, during cell division, the basal bodies that anchor the base of flagellum cannot take up the correct positions that are needed for cell division while remaining attached to a flagellum. This naturally makes the process of cell division clumsier than in unflagellated cells (flagellation constraint).

A larger colony needed more metabolic resources to further reproduce (enlargement constraint). This is essentially logical; it's like saying that if we have more offspring, we need more resources to feed them. If this is the case, why did we become multicellular at all? This was the question that took organisms 1,500 million years to work out. Larger group sizes are beneficial for survival of a colony (especially when predators are present), as well as for fertility (the more offspring, the less overall incidence of defective ones).

The 'fitness' of any population is the product of its viability as a life form and its capacity to reproduce. In unicellular organisms, the same cell must contribute to the two components that measure fitness: bodily functions and reproduction. In multicellular animals, separate cells specialize in reproductive (germ cell) and survival-enhancing (soma or somatic, or structural) functions; such multicellular animals are called metazoans. However, as cells specialize into reproductive germ cells, they relinquish their autonomy in favour of the group. In the case of volvocine algae, while all colonies derived from a single clonal cell, small colonies did not show reproductive functions, unlike larger colonies. This may simply be because it takes two to tango—once a cell has developed specialized reproductive organs, it cannot reproduce on its own. The needs of the colony override individual needs. As a cell was added, changing the volvocine algae's reproductive model, it improved the overall fitness of the group. But as these changes happened gradually, with many colonies 'overlapping', there was no decrease in viability. Because colonies were added gradually, huge additional resources were not needed all at once.

SpongeBob SquarePants, the wildly popular cartoon series that was created by marine biologist Stephen Hillenburg, depicts the marine sponge in the physical shape of a kitchen sponge. Because sponges have not been known to excrete, i.e., when one thinks of a sponge, one thinks of a 'soaking up' action (much like a kitchen sponge, actually), people assumed that sponges did not have 'skin' that made them 'separate and sovereign', unlike more evolved creatures. I was watching an episode of this cartoon with my daughter, and in one scene SpongeBob SquarePants said, 'Isn't this great Squidward? It's just the three of us. You, me and this brick wall you built between us.' Squidward has erected a barricade rather like skin, SpongeBob may have thought. You see, sponges have now been shown to have a distinct outer layer of cells, or an epithelium.

A study of the Great Barrier Reef sponges in Australia shows that they evolved some 635 million years ago, the oldest evidence for multicellular organisms on Earth. Marine sponges provide great insight into the development of both multicellular forms and also the functions of primitive skin. For a start, sponges were ancient animals that diverged along the evolutionary pathway from other unicellular creatures, and went on to become metazoans 600–650 million years ago, even if they shared the characteristics of more primitive forms. Sponges are metazoans, i.e., multicellular members of the animal kingdom, even if they lack typical organs like intestines or nervous systems.

As we discussed earlier, to be considered an organ, a group of cells needs to be organized to perform functions of absorption/ inspiration, metabolism and excretion/expiration.

When Sally Leys and her team at the University of Alberta in Edmonton, Canada, grew flat sponges immersed in liquid, they found that sponge epithelium did keep molecules out, only allowing 0.8 per cent through in three hours. However, sponges are at the very base of the metazoan pyramid; everything higher up is generally considered to be 'anything but a sponge or fungus', i.e., they have true cell organization for different functions. Sponges do not have a nervous system or gut, but they *do* have skin. The sponge's primitive skin performed the function of isolating its interior from the exterior milieu. This barrier allowed cells to communicate without any interference from outside chemicals. The Canadian team's finding confirmed the scientific view that sponges have skin, even if they have no other organs—and this in turn demonstrated that *skin was the first organ to evolve.*

Our understanding of the evolution of an organ is based on the idea that all organs basically develop from simpler forms. In other words, a primitive skin or heart would have to exist for a new skin or heart to develop. The challenge that 'Darwinist' scientists face is that it is hard to find evidence of new organs evolving by 'natural selection'. One of the theories proposed for the evolution of new organs is 'exaptation', the process by which an organ evolves to perform a different role from its original one.

Is all evolution about natural selection or survival of the fittest? Darwin understood that many factors were at work and that natural selection alone could not account for evolutionary changes. He himself said:[12]

> I am convinced that Natural Selection has been the most important, but not the exclusive, means of modification.

The existence of a more advanced organ does not necessarily provide evidence of evolutionary descent. We all know dogs have a more acute sense of smell than humans, but would humans be better off with a dog's sense of smell? It is likely that we'd end up with sensory overload and be unable to function without distraction.

Nicole King, associate professor of genetics, genomics and development at the University of California, Berkeley, is a great expert on single-celled choanoflagellates, which existed long before the evolution of multicellular animals. Surprisingly, she found that one of the most abundant and important cell-adhesion molecules in the animal kingdom, cadherins, existed in these choanoflagellates. Cadherins are long proteins composed of several modules linked together like beads on a string. They extend from the cell and use calcium ions to adhere to adjacent cells. This adhesion is cell-specific—

for instance, it helps nerve cells connect to nerve cells, and skin cells stick to skin cells. Therefore, in animal cells, cadherins help cells stick to their neighbours. So why would primitive single-celled organisms need cadherins? This finding, that a molecule necessary for animals in the future *predated* evolution of the animal itself, makes me marvel at the evolutionary chain of genes that link all creatures.

As a skin cancer researcher, I find the presence of cadherins in unicellular primitive organisms particularly fascinating. Skin cancers like melanomas and squamous cell cancers are often known to metastasize, i.e., spread to other organs through lymphatic channels. As discussed earlier, cadherins function like calcium-dependent 'glue' holding cells together. However, these molecules also make tumour cells stick together. When cadherin function in tumour cells is disturbed, it causes individual tumour cells or clumps of cells to break away. These cell clumps either block off or invade lymphatic and blood channels, with severe clinical implications.

Charles Marshall, director of the University of California's Museum of Palaeontology in Berkeley, has been quoted as saying:[13]

> ...there was an elaborate machinery in place that already had some function. What I want to know now is what were all these genes doing prior to the advent of sponge.

As I was finishing my last operation for the day, a malignant melanoma, I wondered what cadherins were doing *before* cancer was known and organisms had only one cell. As I pondered the evolution of multicellular organisms, it began to seem strangely logical.

When we speak of multicellularity, we are talking about genes that encode the mechanisms of cell division, growth and specialization into different tissues, adhesions and cell death. Obviously, if one of these mechanisms fails, the cells will uncontrollably divide into too many cells of one type. This is essentially what happens in cancer or immune-system diseases. In other words, the very genes that encoded multicellularity had genetic codes to deal with cancers later on, as multicellularity brought with it the risk of more things going wrong, or cells deciding to divide uncontrollably, as happens in tumours. This was why cadherins were present in primitive organisms, as a sort of control mechanism.

A study of the draft genome (genetic information) of the Queensland sponge *Amphimedon queenslandica* confirmed this by showing genes that control cell growth, cell death, cell-to-cell adhesion, developmental signalling and even innate immunity. These genes, necessary for multicellularity, are linked to genes that are disturbed in human cancers (like oncogenes and tumour-suppressor genes).

In the next chapter, we will study the development of skin cells using drosophila, the fruit fly. It is my view that this *sharing of genes* is the real miracle of evolution. In an article titled just that, 'Miracle of Evolution', Stephen M. Barr, theoretical particle physicist and author of *Modern Physics and Ancient Faith*, says:[14]

> In the words of the late Stephen Jay Gould, man has been 'dethroned'. There is no 'ontological discontinuity' (as the late pope called it) between man and the lower animals. We are simply the products of an evolutionary process, and therefore moral concepts based on religion or Natural Law must give way to 'evolutionary ethics' and sociobiology.

Notes

1. Jeremy Bernstein, *Einstein*, Viking Press, 1973, p. 11. Quoted from 'Albert Einstein—There is Neither Evolution Nor Destiny; Only Being', http://www.tm.org/blog/enlightenment/albert-einstein/, accessed 17 March 2012.

2. Darwin quote sourced from Denis O. Lamoureux, 'Theological Insights from Charles Darwin', http://www.asa3.org/ASA/PSCF/2004/PSCF3-04Lamoureux.pdf, accessed 12 March 2012.

3. Stanley L. Miller, 'A production of amino acids under possible primitive earth conditions', *Science*, New Series, Vol. 117, Issue 3046, 15 May 1953, pp. 528–29.

4. N.C. Wickramasinghe and F. Hoyle, 'Miller–Urey Synthesis in the

Nuclei of Galaxies', *Astrophysics and Space Science*, 259: 1998, pp. 99–103.

5. Charles Darwin's letter, as quoted by J.D. Bernal in *The Origin of Life*, Weidenfeld and Nicholson, London, 1967.

6. Karen Bernardo, 'Characterization in Literature', http://learn.lexiconic.net/characters.htm, accessed 17 March 2012.

7. '"Accelerated Evolution" Converts RNA Enzyme to DNA Enzyme In Vitro', *ScienceDaily*, 27 March 2006.

8. Ramachandra Guha, *India After Gandhi: The History of the World's Largest Democracy*, Pan Macmillan, 2008, pp. 769–70.

9. J.B.S. Haldane, 'Data Needed for a Blueprint of the First Organism', in Sidney W. Fox (ed.), *The Origins of Prebiological Systems and of Their Molecular Matrices: Proceedings of a Conference Conducted at Wakulla Springs, Florida, 27–30 October 1963*, Academic Press, New York, 1965, p. 12.

10. Richard Dawkins, *The Blind Watchmaker*, Norton, New York, 1987, p. 139.

11. Dr Oscar Levy (ed.), *The Complete Works of Friedrich Nietzsche: The First Complete and Authorised English Translation (Volume Ten, The Joyful Wisdom)*, The Macmillan Company, New York, 1924.

12. Darwin quoted in Ed Regis, *What Is Life: Investigating the Nature of Life in the Age of Synthetic Biology*, Oxford University Press, 2008, p. 114.

13. Adam Mann, 'Sponge genome goes deep', *Nature*, 466, 673 (2010), published online 4 August 2010.

14. Stephen M. Barr, 'Miracle of Evolution', http://www.columbia.edu/cu/augustine/2006spring/barr_ft.pdf, accessed 12 March 2012.

THREE

Not Birth, Marriage or Death, but Gastrulation

Is the great chain, that draws all to agree,
And drawn supports, upheld by God, or thee?

II

Presumptuous Man! the reason wouldst thou find,
Why form'd so weak, so little, and so blind!
First, if thou canst, the harder reason guess,
Why form'd no weaker, blinder, and no less!
Ask of thy mother earth, why oaks are made
Taller or stronger than the weeds they shade?
Or ask of yonder argent fields above,
Why Jove's Satellites are less than Jove?
Of Systems possible, if 'tis confest
That Wisdom infinite must form the best,
Where all must full or not coherent be,
And all that rises, rise in due degree;
Then, in the scale of reas'ning life, 'tis plain
There must be, somewhere, such rank as Man;
And all the question (wrangle e'er so long)
Is only this, if God has plac'd him wrong?
Respecting Man, whatever wrong we call,
Nay, must be right, as relative to all.

In human works, tho' labour'd on with pain,
A thousand movements scarce one purpose gain;
In God's, one single can its end produce;
Yet serves to second too some other use.
So Man, who here seems principal alone,
Perhaps acts second to some sphere unknown,
Touches some wheel, or verges to some goal;
'Tis but a part we see, and not a whole.
When the proud steed shall know why Man restrains
His fiery course, or drives him o'er the plains;
When the dull Ox, why now he breaks the clod,
Is now a victim, and now Egypt's God:
Then shall Man's pride and dullness comprehend
His actions', passions', being's use and end;
Why doing, suff'ring, check'd, impell'd; and why
This hour a slave, the next a deity.
Then say not Man's imperfect, Heav'n in fault;
Say rather, Man's as perfect as he ought;
His knowledge measur'd to his state and place,
His time a moment, and a point his space.
If to be perfect in a certain sphere,
What matter, soon or late, or here or there?
The blest today is as completely so,
As who began a thousand years ago.

– Alexander Pope, 'Essay on Man'[1]

If you think about it, the ocean isn't condemned as evil because some ship sinks in it. The ocean surrounds ships, that's what oceans do. Rather like how skin surrounds the other organs and cells in our body. But everyone has some issue with their skin, be it a concern with tanning, ageing, pigmentation, acne or skin cancer. The problem with ramparts is that they are built not just to keep things out, but also to see what or who is capable of breaching them. What we need then is to understand the function and metabolism of skin. But to understand our skin, we need to know its history—which is why we need to take in *this* story.

The Development of Human Skin

Skin, as I said earlier, is the largest organ in the human body, with a surface area of around 2m². Its thickness varies from 0.5mm on our eyelids to 4mm or more on the soles of our feet. About 16 per cent of our body weight is made up of skin. We know now that primitive sponges had 'skin', but being marine creatures, their skin was not called upon to perform the roles of UV and sun protection. So as animal skin evolved, it took on additional functions that were necessary in non-marine environments.

As we briefly discussed earlier, skin essentially has two layers: epidermis and dermis.

The surface layer, the epidermis, contains cells called keratinocytes, which migrate up from the basal layer and create the epidermis, a 'dead' (devoid of blood supply) layer. It acts as a wall and prevents the entry of bacteria/microbes, while also preventing the loss of essential water, electrolytes and proteins.

The dermis, or the deeper skin layer, has hair follicles, sweat glands, oil glands and collagen. It maintains strength and elasticity, and regulates temperature via blood vessels and sweat glands.

The epidermis and dermis develop from a single layer of embryonic 'multi-potent progenitor stem cells' (simply put, stem cells that are capable of differentiating into multiple forms). What this means is that, in the embryo, these keratinocyte stem cells receive signals from the environment that cause them to differentiate, i.e., develop into tissues like epidermis, hair follicles or sebaceous glands. As we grow into adults, we continue to be subjected to daily assaults from the environment, like sun damage, cuts and bruises. Skin and hair follicles are constantly being repaired by a process controlled by adult stem cells. Where do these adult stem cells come from? Are their numbers determined at the embryonic stage itself? When an injury occurs, how do these cells decide how many cells to produce and of what type?

During the stage of embryo development in animals, a single-layered blastula rearranges itself into a three-layered gastrula by a process of cell migration, as in Figure 8. This creates a gastrula, which has three germ cell layers: ectoderm, mesoderm and endoderm.

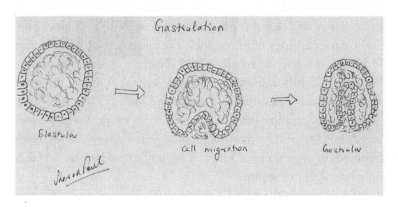

FIGURE 8   Stages of embryo development

It is not birth, marriage, or death, but gastrulation, which is truly the most important time in your life.

– Lewis Wolpert[2]

These are oft-quoted words from Lewis Wolpert, developmental biologist and author of *Principles of Development* (Oxford University Press, 1997). The gastrulation stage is important because thence follows organ development. The epidermis develops from the outer ectodermal layer (some people refer to this layer as 'neuroectoderm', as it also gives rise to the neural crest, and therefore nerves), while the dermis, which contains blood vessels and hair follicles, develops from the middle mesodermal layer. In general, structures that give architectural strength are derived from the mesoderm. The endoderm usually develops into internal, especially digestive, organs.

If the outer layer, the neuroectoderm, gives rise to both epidermis and nerves, how does it decide *when* to produce skin rather than nerve cells?

There is a raging debate on whether gastrulation studies ought to focus on a few 'model organisms', which means that scientists would apply the laws of probability to their understanding of processes. Given that many common genetic signals are involved in gastrulation, and that it is not humanly possible to understand the evolutionary biology of every single organism, scientists argue that focusing on a few organisms would illustrate common processes better. Drosophila, the fruit fly (*see plate section*), is one of the most studied 'model organisms' in genetics and biology. This is because it is a hardy creature, easy to care for with minimal equipment, breeds quickly and lays many eggs. *Drosophila melanogaster* produces hundreds of eggs after just one mating, and a new generation takes only two weeks to appear.

Interestingly, in the 2008 US presidential elections, research using the drosophila attracted the interest of Sarah Palin, who was John McCain's vice-presidential candidate. Sarah Palin ridiculed fruit-fly research saying:[3]

> … sometimes these dollars go to projects that have little or nothing to do with the public good. Things like fruit-fly research in Paris, France. I kid you not.

Her ridiculing tone attracted the ire of geneticists, as the fruit fly is indispensable to the study of genetics and evolution, given that, as we have seen, many creatures share genes.

Jumping to the defence of the fruit fly, well-known geneticist Professor Jerry Coyne wrote to the *Philadelphia Inquirer*, pointing out that the fruit fly is what the geneticists call a 'model organism'. Fundamentally, all organisms share an evolutionary pathway. The biochemistry, development of tissues and their regulation by genes are common to most organisms. Given this context, the fruit fly is an ideal organism because it breeds quickly and is easy to study. And, as the good professor pointed out, there are many more fruit flies than there are chimps, they are not endangered and they are much cheaper to study than mice.

Research into inherited genetic diseases, such as Down's syndrome, which have specific chromosomal abnormalities, would not have been possible but for the fruit fly. The fruit fly has been responsible for no less than four Nobel Prizes (the first of which was awarded to T.H. Morgan in 1933), and is today being used as a model for the study of both Alzheimer's disease and autism.

I can vouch for the fact that the humble fruit fly is indispensable in our study of the development of skin and the 'Wnt signalling pathway'. I'll pause to explain this because it's important. 'Wnt' is an ancient genetic signal. (A 'signal' is essentially a network of proteins that regulates a particular pathway; and a 'pathway' is the circuitry that leads to the development of a particular tissue following a genetic signal.) The Wnt signal has been preserved over time, and plays an important role in both the formation of the embryo as well as in the development of cancer.

About 25 years ago, Int1 or Integration 1, the first identified gene to encode a signalling component, was discovered in mouse tumour cells. Around the same time, the gene 'Wingless' was found in *Drosophila melanogaster*, which we commonly know as a 'fruit fly'. Wingless, as the name indicates, produced developmental wing defects in the fruit fly embryo. Wnt is essentially a scientific combination of the words Wingless and Int1.

What does the network of proteins that constitute the Wnt signalling pathway actually do? To start with, the Wnt signal stops cells from responding to 'fibroblast growth factors' (FGF; fibroblasts are cells that produce collagen and structural tissue; however, FGF are a family of polypeptides that help in the production of blood vessels, wound healing and embryo development). It makes them respond to bone morphogenetic proteins (BMP; these growth factors were originally thought to induce production of bone and cartilage and hence the name[4]), thus leading to the development of epidermal cells.

Conversely, in the absence of the Wnt signalling pathway, the ectoderm receives cues from FGF and inhibits BMP, and so the embryo ends up producing nerve cells instead. Thus, the initial production of the epidermal skin layer (or nerves) instead of the embryo is the result of a response to this Wnt signal (*see Figure 9*). When the Wnt signalling pathway is absent, the ectoderm receives its cues from FGF and inhibits BMP, and so the embryo produces nerve cells instead.

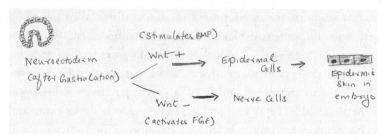

FIGURE 9   **Wnt and its role in producing epidermal or, alternately, nerve cells**

The single layer of embryonic epidermal cells thus formed, in turn, may or may not themselves express Wnt signals.

Some of the cells that *fail* to respond to Wnt end up producing more layers of epidermal cells and this resultant multilayered epidermis is then said to be 'stratified'—a process modulated via the BMP and the notch signalling system. (The notch signal was so named because this genetic signalling pathway was noted to cause a 'notch' in the wing of the fruit fly.)

However, sometimes these cells *do* respond to the Wnt signalling pathway, and then go on to receive FGF signals and inhibit BMP signals instead, and together they end up producing a skin appendage, such as a sweat gland. In conjunction with early epidermal signals, as illustrated in Figure 10, the ectodermal Wnt signals instruct the epidermis to grow downwards and form a hair bud or placode (an area of thickening in the embryonic epithelial layer where some organ or structure later develops).

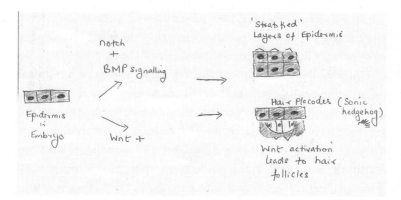

FIGURE 10   Epidermal genetic signals leading to
multilayers or hair follicle production

'Wait a minute,' I hear you say, 'isn't this the reverse response to Wnt?'

This confusion is only to be expected because the human mind easily comprehends the theory, but not the 'smartness' of the genetic tools that nature employs. This is why, even though there are hundreds of genes associated with the development of skin, to avoid confusing readers further, I am only discussing a few key ones in this book.

In linguistics, 'portmanteau' is a term used to denote the combination of two words to make up a third; common examples are smog (smoke and fog) or motel (motor inn and hotel). In 1956, Herbert A. Simon came up with a portmanteau combining 'satisfy' and 'suffice': satisfice.[5] Simon felt that human minds are reliant on memory and therefore unreliable. It is difficult for us to know the results of our actions in the future with precision. Therefore, we rationalize things, i.e., we say, '... given the time and money available, this is the best decision we can make.' Spoken like a true economist? Herbert A. Simon was one.

But if we could foretell the outcome of our actions, we'd be satisfied that our decisions were optimal and sufficient; we'd rest 'satisficed'. Remember Haldane's discussion on 'probability limits'? Organs and organisms in nature seem to have an innate knowledge of outcomes that are beyond what we can fathom.

Lewis Wolpert, the 'father of gastrulation', speaks of 'positional information and value'—cells seem to do the right thing in the right place, modulated by genetic codes and molecules that are the same across many species, tissues and stages in development. Lewis Wolpert uses the 'French Flag' model (even if he was originally from South Africa) to explain the action of morphogens. A morphogen is a signalling molecule that acts on cells, but the effect it causes is based on its concentration. Well-known genetic morphogens are Wingless/Wnt and Sonic Hedgehog/SHH, which is another signal discussed below. (See *plate section* for my adaptation of Wolpert's model.)

On the blue-white-red model, high concentrations of a morphogen activate a blue gene, low concentrations activate a white gene, and red is the default state, where concentration is too low to cause any activity.

The French Flag model explains why, in the beginning, Wnt signals caused the ectoderm to respond to BMP and produce skin cells, but once the epidermal layer is established, it inhibits BMP. This is all to do with the *concentration* of the molecules concerned— at different concentrations of a signal, the effects are different.

Gene names often have interesting origins. Just over two decades ago, in 1991, Sega, a maker of computer games released *Sonic The Hedgehog* (the company even registered 'The' as Sonic's middle name) to compete with Nintendo's Mario.

Sonic Hedgehog, the gaming character, is essentially a humanoid hedgehog who curls up to form a ball and attacks enemies at supersonic speeds. In 2008, *The Telegraph* reported a poll that revealed Sonic Hedgehog to be the most popular video game character in the world—ahead of Lara Croft of *Tomb Raider*, who was made popular by Angelina Jolie in a film by the same name. We're interested in him here because Sonic Hedgehog also went on to inspire the naming of a major embryonic gene that is especially important for skin and hair development.

The 'Sonic Hedgehog gene' (SHH) is one of the early genes expressed by the placodes, essentially pre-buds of tissue. While ectodermal Wnt signals instruct epidermal cells to form a hair follicle, SHH has a crucial role in developing deeper, i.e., dermal, cells to form a hair follicle. When drosophila was genetically modified to lack this SHH gene, it developed spines like a hedgehog. This gene has also been found in some spiky mammals like the Indian hedgehog and the desert hedgehog. This conflicting action is again explained by the fact that the SHH gene has a dual action: in low concentrations, it tends to produce more cells, but in higher concentrations, tends to inhibit cellular proliferation (another example of the French Flag model).

The Sonic Hedgehog gene is not only responsible for hair follicle formation, but also for the spacing between hairs and hair growth after birth. When humans have defective SHH genes, unlike the fruit fly, they don't just develop spiky skin, they can also develop skin tumours, like basal cell cancers (BCC).

BCCs are the most common skin cancers (around 70–80 per cent of all skin cancers), and their worldwide incidence is increasing. They can be both single invasive tumours, or scattered over the body like naevi (which is the medical term for skin moles), the 'basal cell naevus syndrome' (described first by Gorlin). Genetic studies on patients with basal cell naevus syndrome indicate that faults in the regulation of the SHH signal in epidermal keratinocytes are primarily responsible for the development of BCC.

Our key understanding from all of this is that, when skin layers are developed, the interaction of SHH proteins lays down a basic body pattern. The consequences of a mutation in the Sonic Hedgehog gene in humans are very serious indeed. Most of the time, the embryo simply doesn't survive because its body layout is completely disordered. If the embryo manages to survive, it usually has major problems with skin, brain and facial development.

When I teach cutaneous surgery, I stress the importance of closing the deeper layers of skin, i.e., the dermal layer. If you simply suture the skin surface, you do not support the wound with enough mechanical strength. Those who don't specifically train in surgery may not have learnt this. Therefore, many doctors with no formal surgical training routinely close cutaneous wounds with a single layer, and without the use of long-lasting deeper sutures to approximate the deep dermal layer. So, after the skin sutures are removed, the wound pulls apart over time to leave a wide scar.

One of the questions we ask while teaching cutaneous surgery is this: what is the tensile strength of a sutured wound (when compared to normal) after a week (when sutures are usually removed)? Answer: 3 to 5 per cent.

Most students (and patients) might assume that a sutured wound would be at least 50 per cent as strong as undamaged skin. But in actual fact, skin edges following surgery and after suture removal retain only 3 to 5 per cent of the tensile strength of normal tissue. This is why it is important to support deeper tissue with the use of absorbable sutures. It is also important to educate patients by explaining that they need to, for a while, avoid activities that may cause tension across the wound surface.

In the human body, tissues that are derived from mesoderm form the support structures. In skin, this is the dermis, making it vitally important from a surgical point of view. The epidermis, on the other hand, is important as a barrier. Naturally, the epidermis must be linked with the immune system, so it too can fight infection when injury occurs. Too little production of epidermal cells would result in thinning of skin (as happens with age), and too much can cause excessive skin build-up as happens in diseases like psoriasis or cancer. This would explain why cancers and psoriasis sometimes occur over injured sites—it is essentially a failure of repair mechanisms. So how is this skin repair controlled?

When the body sustains an injury, like when we fall over and break skin, the epidermis needs to do two things: firstly, develop an immune response and fight infections, and secondly, activate the wound repair mechanism. But, of course, this mechanism needs to *know* it has produced enough cells, and stop producing more, through some kind of genetic feedback mechanism.

For a start, the basal cell layer of the epidermis (where the BCC arise) relies on an underlying basement membrane, which functions rather like a scaffold that is rich in extra-cellular matrix proteins and growth factors. Basal cells attach themselves to this frame-like structure using two types of adhesive links, both composed of integrins. Integrins are also useful in cell growth and migration, and therefore essential for wound repair. (For example, cells lacking a $\alpha\beta_1$ integrins are less migratory, whereas those lacking $\alpha_6\beta_4$ integrins show more mobility.)

However, to function as a tissue, basal cells need to adhere to one another and therefore communicate with each other. Remember how organisms evolved from having one cell to many cells and the role of cadherins? No surprise then that basal cells adhere to one another using 'adherens junctions', the core of which is a cadherin protein called E-cadherin. To adhere to other basal cells, E-cadherin binds two related proteins, β-catenin and $_p$120 catenin.

Researchers believe that these adherens junctions work like crowd-control mechanisms. When the epidermis is damaged, a reduction in adherens junctions makes cells migrate and proliferate. Once the repair is complete, these systems return to normal. However, when the circuitry goes awry, too much cell proliferation can result. The clinical consequences of defects in the expression of the E-cadherin–catenin cell adhesion complex are particularly severe: the epidermis develops extremely invasive tumours like squamous cell cancers, especially on the head and neck. (To illustrate the severity of the clinical consequence, I have included two photographs from a tumour I operated on recently in the *plate section.*)

Skin is a barrier, rather like a brick wall, and the lipid layer is like the mortar that holds bricks together. We have just discussed the role of cadherins in adherens junctions and integrins in creating this brick wall. But how do these cells build the brick wall to the architect's plan and create different shapes? In this context, we need to understand that epidermal cells show both symmetrical and asymmetrical divisions.

Essentially, the first step for symmetrical development is 'stratification', or the formation of new layers. As we discussed earlier, BMP and notch signals play a major role in this pathway. But in the main, epidermal cells preserve their ability for cell division by mitosis—all the while maintaining links with the basement membranes, the thin sheets of protein fibres that separate the epithelium from the underlying tissue. And, as we have discussed, this is regulated by adhesion complexes, including integrins. The second step is 'differentiation' by delamination, where the cells detach themselves from the basement membrane and layer themselves in organized rows one on top of another. This method leads to symmetrical epidermal proliferation.

When the epidermis proliferates in an asymmetrical fashion, the first step is the same, i.e., stratification. However, rather than delamination or detachment from the basement membrane, the cellular contents are asymmetrically partitioned into two daughter cells.

Epidermis can actually be built and maintained by either of these two mechanisms. In keeping with the French Flag model, a study of mice skin and delamination found that the cells with the highest integrin levels have the best attachment and proliferation potential, whereas those with low integrin levels detach from the basement membrane and differentiate into other cells. Studies on the fruit fly show asymmetrical proliferation. A study of the fruit fly's neuroblasts, or embryonic nerve cells, found that the cell partitions its contents into two daughter cells. A basal transcription factor, $_p63$, has been shown to be responsible for epidermal stratification.(A transcription factor is essentially a protein that binds to a specific DNA segment during transcription, the process by which genetic information flows from DNA to mRNA.) In the absence of the $_p63$ transcription factor, basal cells seem capable of only symmetrical division. In the fruit fly, notch signalling controls the machinery of asymmetrical division.

These skin genetic signalling proteins and the development of epidermis from the ectoderm reveal that the skin is a rich source of readily available stem cells. Understanding and using them is the *future* of cutaneous medicine and surgery (or indeed future treatments for cancer or paralysis). While the main purpose of stem cells was originally to maintain and replenish body tissues, increasingly, harvesting these stem cells allows us to 'manufacture' replacement skin or nerve cells.

From a skin point of view, the hair follicle stem cell niche is a key reservoir for skin stem cells. And the key component of the hair follicle is the 'bulge'.

To get our heads around the 'battle of the bulge' from the stem cell perspective, we need to understand the cyclical nature of hair follicles. The hair follicle (*see Figure 11*) is one of the few organs that undergo degeneration and regeneration throughout the course of an organism's life. Hair follicles grow in stages:

1. Follicular, or the development stage: when the hair follicle is formed.
2. Anagen, or the growth phase of hair: on an average, this is two to three years for scalp hair and three years for eyebrow hair.
3. Catagen, or the regressing phase of hair: this is when hair regresses or involutes (no connection with receding hair, as we are discussing individual hair follicles here and not hair patterns); on average two to three weeks.

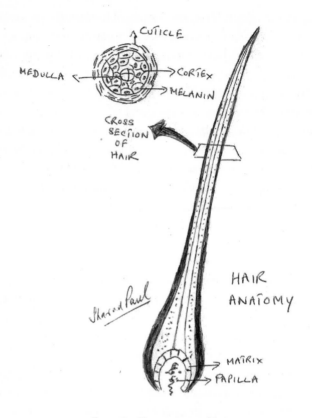

FIGURE 11   The anatomy of hair

4. Telogen, or the resting phase of hair: on average two to three months for scalp hair and around nine months for eyebrow hair. (Fortunately, eyebrow hair has a long resting period, or one's eyebrows may have ended up as long as scalp hair!)

5. Exogen, or shedding phase: this happens when several hairs arise from one hair follicle ('twinning'), and some of these are discarded.

When the telogen, or resting phase, is more prominent, there are not enough cells in the anagen, or growth phase, and this leads to baldness. This tends to run in families and male-pattern baldness is often inherited. Even though some people manage to grow hair to lengths below their waistlines, every individual has a 'hair cycle limit', i.e., a point at which 90 per cent of their hair has reached maximal length. For scalp hair, it is on average three to four years (of course there are individual variations for anything). This is true even for eyebrow hair: usually, an average of four to six months. If you see older people with really bushy eyebrows, this is not because their hair is longer, but because it is denser, not having been plucked.

At the onset of the anagen phase, the 'recycling' portion of the hair follicle regenerates and initiates a new round of hair growth. This regeneration requires stem cells, which reside in the lowest permanent part of the hair follicle. As there is already an existing hair in the follicle, the production of new cells leads to a 'bulge', i.e., an extra layer of cells that will keep the follicle from bulging once the existing hair is shed. This bulge area is very important in stem cell research as it contains cells that are maintained (by genetic signals) in a 'quiet', undifferentiated state or milieu ('differentiation' is when cells develop into different cell types—therefore, undifferentiated cells can morph into any type of cell). (*See Figure 12*). This bulge area is, therefore, the subject of intense studies in stem cell research worldwide.

Normally, cells in the hair follicle are maintained in an undifferentiated quiescent state. So, self-renewal factors control renewal of hair follicles, and the differentiation-inhibitory factors stop cells from evolving into new cell types. However, in stem cell research, the exciting aspect is that these 'bulge cells' can be mobilized to replenish the cells of the sebaceous gland and/or epidermis when needed.

One of the findings in developmental biology is that these embryonic epithelial cells are actually responsive even in other areas, like mesenchyme. (Mesenchyme is connective tissue, which like bones and muscles, is mostly derived from mesoderm. In our earlier discussion of gastrulation, we learnt that ectoderm produces epidermis or nerve cells, depending on the signals it receives.) For

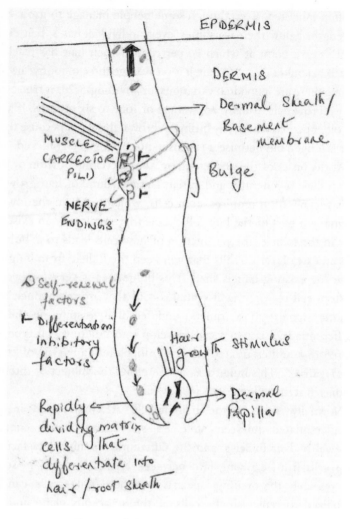

FIGURE 12   **Bulge cells and cell differentiation**

example, in an experiment where the epidermis of the leg was confronted with chicken wing mesenchymal cells, it produced feathers. This astonishing ability to morph into other cell types seems to be confined to these bulge cells. Obviously, people running hair-loss clinics are already harvesting these cells, and keratinocytes are already cultured to treat burns. But think of this: if we exposed a bulge cell to cornea, it may produce corneal cells, which could treat certain types of blindness; or if they produced nerve cells, they could be used to treat paralysis. Many stem cell researchers are already excited, and are testing stem cells harvested from the bulge area of the hair follicle.

But that isn't the only part of the skin's landscape that has been exciting researchers. Remember the Sonic Hedgehog signal we discussed earlier and its role in basal cell skin cancers? Researchers have found that it determines why our pinky is the fifth finger and not our thumb. In other words, the SHH gene is necessary in the ectoderm for normal limb and digit formation. Studies in mice have shown that if we get rid of or suppress the SHH signal in the ectoderm, an extra digit forms. This has caused a rethink of not only development of limbs and digits, but also of the potential applications of this discovery in the future.

An extra thumb, anyone? Or maybe settle for baby-like skin at the age of 100? These may seem like museum curiosities, but the genetic signalling apparatus does seem to behave like an experienced museum curator—with a strong desire to fill in gaps and make better collections, yet tempered by the 'satisficing' knowledge that helps optimal decision making.

NOTES

1. Alexander Pope, 'Essay on Man': University of Tennessee Notes: https://notes.utk.edu/bio/greenberg.nsf/11b7b90a9fa8e19585256c 76000ed30a/a41ea6f017abe5b485256db100676048?OpenDocument, accessed 23 August 2012.
2. Lewis Wolpert quoted in 'Darwin 200: Beneath the Surface', *Nature* 456, 2008, pp. 300–03.
3. Sarah Palin, quoted in Jerry Coyne, 'Swatting attacks on fruit flies and science', *The Philadelphia Inquirer*, 31 October 2008, http:// richarddawkins.net/articles/3293, accessed 17 March 2012.
4. Bone morphogenetic proteins were originally named by orthopaedic

surgeon Dr Marshall Urist who discovered that 'dead' bone, when implanted in other tissues, could stimulate bone production due to the presence of certain 'bone growth factors'. However, this BMP family now includes cytokines, which are involved in immune-system modulation.

5. H.A. Simon, 'Rational choice and the structure of the environment', *Psychological Review*, Vol. 63, No. 2, 1956, pp. 129–38: 'Evidently, organisms adapt well enough to "satisfice"; they do not, in general, "optimize".'

FOUR

Rotting Sharks, Smoking Volcanoes and a Deadly Endgame

...Islands exert a special lure for men, and few among us have not at times allowed our thoughts to sail, like a windjammer in the trades, to make landfalls on fabled islands in distant waters. They are evolutionary laboratories where the evidence for organic evolution is often more apparent than it is on continents.

– Charles R. Bennett[1]

The first time I visited Iceland, to speak at the Nordic Plastic Surgery Congress, it was soon after the volcano EyjafjallajÖkull (pronounced AY-uh-fyat-luh-YOE-kuutl-a) erupted in 2010, creating havoc for airlines over several parts of Europe. The uncertainty about travel plans was dwarfed only by the unease surrounding Iceland's economic future. Yet, a remote island always holds a lure for a scientific mind. What would Iceland's animals teach me about the biography of skin? Could it become my very own Galapagos? Even though my travel agent warned me that I would not get any travel insurance cover, I hastily accepted the invitation.

While there were no definite plans in place for this book, I had been researching skin evolution for years—and Iceland could shine a light on that world, I believed. I began to see my trip as a chance to peer through the telescope of comparative evolutionary biology.

When I first stepped out of the airport at Reykjavik, in June 2010, I thought that Armageddon had hit while I was on the long flight from the southern hemisphere. It looked apocalyptic; a veil of fog unfurled from the Arctic and draped over black volcanic sand dunes that belonged in a lunar landscape. The memory of trees back home in New Zealand was still foremost in my mind as I tugged the warm beanie over my forehead and opened the car window to inhale the Arctic air. I was in Iceland. I was here to present my new skin grafting operation, the halo graft, to the plastic surgery world.

It was summer in Reykjavik. I hurried into the lobby of the Grand Hotel at five past midnight. Outside, the sun still shone bright on the walls of the hotel; the lighting inside was artificial and the smiles eerily bright. Or perhaps it was the other way around? The sign on the wall still listed a price reminiscent of the not-long-gone financial

FIGURE 13   The post volcanic-eruption apocalyptic
landscape of Iceland

boom time. The economic crash had hit Iceland hard and all of a sudden. I guess the hotel had not even had time to change the sign.

The attendant was matter of fact: 'It was a stupid idea on the part of the government … they were trying to make Iceland another Switzerland or Monaco without realizing that we are the New Zealand of the North Pole,' she said. 'No one ever goes to New Zealand unless you are already going to see the kangaroos in Australia. See, the last three islands to be inhabited on Earth were New Zealand, Madagascar and Iceland. And there is good reason for that!' She was evidently proud of her knowledge of geography. 'Where did you fly here from?'

'New Zealand,' I said.

'No way!'

'Yes way.'

'Your passport says you were born in England.'

'True.'

'You were born in England and have come to speak at the Nordic Plastic Surgery Conference being held here?'

'Yes, yes.'

'And you live in New Zealand?'

'Yes, although I divide my time between New Zealand and Australia.'

'Why?'

The strongly expressed surprise in her question stumped me. I struggled to answer the question—something I'm ashamed to admit to. The hotel key still serves as a reminder.

The next morning, I found myself eating breakfast alone. That would be unheard of at an Australian conference. I'm not sure who felt more uncomfortable, me stuck at a table all by myself, or the groups at the other tables. Finns, Norwegians, Swedes, Dutch—each at their own tables. The hostess probably felt that she couldn't join any of those tables, or even the lone Antipodean, to avoid insulting any of us.

'How are you today?' the young waitress asked me in precise, halting English.

'Great. I'm feeling like a Jamaican at the winter games in *Cool Runnings*.'

'What's *Cool Runnings*?'

'Never mind. I'll have a coffee, please.'

Finally, it was the morning of my presentation. The conference organizers had put up a poster announcing my talk, 'A New Technique of Skin Grafting—Introducing the Halo Graft in 2010'.

The opening address was by the former president of Iceland, who has a place in history as the world's first elected female president, Vigdís Finnbogadóttir.

Icelandic children have a unique tradition of deriving their surname from the first name of their father. So my daughter's surname would be Sharadsdóttir (Sharad's daughter) and not Paul. She would always remain Sharadsdóttir, and not take her future husband's surname, which would, of course, be derived from his father's given name (for example, if his father's first name was Eric, he would be Ericsson). Doting dads everywhere would approve of the system, I reckon.

But to come back to Madame Vigdís, her address was precise and concise—typically Nordic. She spoke of the friendships between Nordic countries, and noted the historical fact that Greenland gets its name from an attempt to woo people to settle there, instead of Iceland. See, Iceland is warmer than Greenland, which is hardly green, she pointed out.

During a break for lunch, an Icelandic surgeon sat beside me and told me about Icelandic volcanoes. 'There are many eruptions or new ideas in science,' he said to me, 'some have too little lava to make a mark, but during some eruptions, the ground is marked forever. Your skin grafting idea is very simple, but like a good volcanic eruption ... indelible,' he said. I didn't know what to say. The Jamaican *has* made the finals, I thought.

I remember walking past a white townhouse-like building with security guards on all sides. It looked like a large residence, so I asked one of the guards what the building was. He struggled to find the word and asked a colleague. 'It's where government works,' she explained. Iceland has the world's oldest parliament—Alþingi (pronounced Althingi), established in AD 930 by the Vikings. I have a few photographs of the monument. It was impossible, though, to compose a frame without inadvertently capturing some of the many Japanese tourists in Iceland.

I walked past rows of interconnected houses, with only the colours of the walls differentiating them. There were many shops selling Icelandic souvenirs made of volcanic rock. The air was icy, even in summer. The wind chased me, smothering imaginary grass around my feet. Footsteps sounded in the apartments above the shops. I leant close to a window and peered inside a shop selling Arctic fox pelts. The eyes of the fox seemed to follow me and I thought I saw curiosity in its lifeless eyes—the same kind of curiosity with which I viewed Iceland, an almost unique place to study evolutionary biology, especially the biography of skin.

Restaurateurs were putting out boards, with specials of the day handwritten on them. Almost all restaurants had a 'whale menu' and a 'puffin menu' (*see Figure 14*). I remember thinking it rather cute. 'Back home we just call the meals "mains size" and "entrée size",' I told a man who was busy writing on the blackboard. He looked at me quizzically.

I pointed to the 'puffin menu'.

'Oh, puffin. That's the national bird of Iceland.'

'You don't mean ...'

'You don't eat whale or puffin?' He looked at me with some disdain. 'Where are you from?'

'New Zealand.'

'You don't eat your national bird?'

'Are you crazy? Our national bird, the Kiwi, is endangered and rather timid. You'd be sent to prison for longer than if you killed a man.'

FIGURE 14 Yes, they really will serve you whale

He laughed dismissively. 'About twenty years ago, the last fin whale was sighted off the course of Iceland. Fin whales had not been seen for decades. We all rushed and managed to catch the whale. The restaurant across the road put the whale in a giant freezer, and for several years, we could sample fin whale. Now we can only eat minke whales.'

Whether his story was accurate or not, I was amazed at how easily whale meat is available in Iceland. I had a Japanese surgeon friend many years ago. He used to tell me that as a child he had seen whale meat in the Osaka markets. But by the time he was an adult, whale meat was so scarce due to international pressure that the best one could hope for was an occasional tiny can of the stuff. *Now* I know what the Japanese tourists go to Iceland for: their version of culinary research.

Back at the hotel, I read the *New Zealand Herald* online. Pete Bethune, a Kiwi, was on trial in Japan for boarding a Japanese whaling ship armed with a knife and rancid butter. I began to feel sorry for the Japanese. I entered a steak house. All the steaks there were whale steaks—no other meat choices. The menu was unreadable and devoid of vowels, but probably said, 'Eat whale or starve.'

'How does one eat whale?' I asked.

The waitress looked at me like I was a fool before she understood what I was asking. 'Medium,' she said, helpfully.

A few minutes later, I was looking at a large slab of whale meat. Whale tastes like salty beef. It seemed strangely logical. There is hardly any grass in the countryside in Iceland for cattle to graze, and whale babies are called calves.

Whales are one of evolution's great mysteries. Whales and horses first appeared in the Eocene Epoch about 34 to 55 million years ago; this was just before the Ice Age. After taking all the trouble of adapting to dry land, these mammals decided life was better in water after all. But when whales decided to become marine creatures once again, they required many adaptations for their return to water: nostrils that slanted backwards with coverings, change of forelimbs into flippers, loss of hair and the addition of insulating blubber. To me, their skin adaptations are the most interesting.

Philip Gingerich of the University of Michigan has been instrumental in solving the mystery of whale evolution by digging up fossils in Pakistan. *Whales in Pakistan?* It is actually not as far-fetched as it sounds. (Knowing the intense rivalry between India and Pakistan, I'm sure Indian scientists will show me proof that India harboured a few cetaceans too!)

From the Age of Dinosaurs to the Age of Mammals, a period stretching across 500 million years, the Sea of Tethys extended from Spain to Indonesia. At this time, the continental plates moved and the Indian subcontinental plate slammed into the central Asian plate, creating the Himalayas by brute force, and Africa crashed into Europe, creating the Alps.

Warm and shallow, the Sea of Tethys was inviting for creatures, and some mammals, like primitive whales, decided to return to water rather than live on land. In 1979, Philip Gingerich led an international team to Pakistan to study the Kuldana Formation for early fossils from the Sea of Tethys. They found a 52-million-year-old skull of an archaeocete, a kind of primitive whale. These primitive whales had a dense tympanic bone for hearing, but lacked a blowhole like modern whales. They named this creature 'Pakicetus'. Palaeontologists have long believed that, at some stage, whales would have developed primitive feet and hind limbs because they had decided to live on land. Indeed, 10 million years later, Prozeuglodon, an archaeocete found in Egypt showed a well-developed vertebral column and hind limbs, confirming the evolution of whales from land-dwellers back to ocean-dwellers. It was not until the seventeenth century that John Ray suggested that whales be 'ordered' in biological nomenclature as mammals, rather than fish, due to the presence of lungs, not gills.

Their change of habitat, naturally, also needed modification of the skin. To understand the adaptation of whale skin to marine life, we need to look at the normal structure of mammalian or human skin. We know now that the epidermis develops from the ectoderm, while the dermis develops from the mesoderm. The epidermis is what we refer to biologically as the epithelium, which means it has no blood vessels or nerves, and serves as lining tissue. No blood vessels course through the epidermis, nor do any nerves make themselves felt. These structures are located in the deeper skin layer, the dermis. The dermis is part of what we refer to as connective tissue, so it can produce blood vessels and serve as the source of nutrition as well as a reservoir of waste for the deep epidermal cells.

Epithelial cells like the epidermis have great powers of regeneration, and are therefore constantly flaking off and being renewed. It is estimated that humans lose around 200g of skin each day. Accessory structures like hair and glands lie in the dermis, even though (as we saw in the previous chapter) they are of ectodermal and, therefore, epidermal origin. This is why hair follicles and glands can also regenerate themselves—it is a feature of their origins in epithelium.

The dermis that lies beneath the epidermis, on the other hand, has blood vessels and nerves, as well as lymphatic channels. These blood vessels form capillary loops near the epidermis and help in clearing metabolic waste. What we call 'subcutis' or subcutaneous tissue in humans is sometimes referred to as the hypodermis; this is the layer just below the dermis, and technically, just below the skin. This is where the term 'hypodermic' needle came from, as needles for injection are normally positioned just below the skin or into muscle. Needles that penetrate the dermis can be especially painful, because the connective tissue here has very tight spaces and more dense nerve endings.

The structures of the epidermis are really an expression of the keratinizing cells of the skin. Around 95 per cent of cells in the epidermis are keratinocytes, i.e., cells that contain keratin, which is a protein that also makes up other epithelial derivatives like nails and hair. The remaining 5 per cent of cells are melanocytes, i.e., cells that contain melanin, the pigment that determines skin colour. As discussed in the previous chapter on stratification of epidermal layers, keratinocytes are constantly produced in the deeper layers of the epidermis by mitosis and rapidly ascend, to be replaced by a new wave of keratinocytes. The 'lifespan' of a keratinocyte is about a week, which means that the epidermal layers reflect different life stages of keratinocytes.

The deepest layer of the epidermis is the basal layer, or the *stratum basale*, which is single-layered. This is the 'factory' of keratinocytes, where cells divide both symmetrically and asymmetrically. The layer above the basal layer is the *stratum spinosum*, or the spinous layer; the spiny look is due to the intercellular bridges or junctions (desmosomes) that hold cells together. At this stage, the cells are 'nearly dead'—that is, they are still capable of division, an ability they lose as they migrate further upwards. The layer above this is the *stratum granulosum*, or the granular layer, so named due to the presence of granules like keratohyalin, which promote both hydration of skin and interconnections of keratin. By this stage, the keratinocytes are considered 'dead', as they can no longer divide. In areas like palms and soles, we also have a clear or translucent epidermal layer, called *stratum lucidum*, just above the granular layer. The uppermost layer of epidermis is the *stratum corneum*, or horny layer, which contains corneocytes (keratinocytes that have lost cell nucleus and cytoplasm, and developed thickened envelopes and aggregates of hard keratin). These corneocytes (*see Figure 15*) contain about 80 per cent keratin and can be found in layers that are more than ten cells thick. The corneocyte formation process is rather like watching a juicy grape become a raisin.

With that, we return to the skin adaptation of whales. The fascinating thing about whale skin is that it *does not* develop a *stratum granulosum* (the granular cell layer). Rather, the process of keratinization takes a more primitive form in which the cells of the *stratum corneum* retain their nuclei. This results in the uppermost horny layer of cells retaining a flattened nucleus, a condition we call parakeratosis.

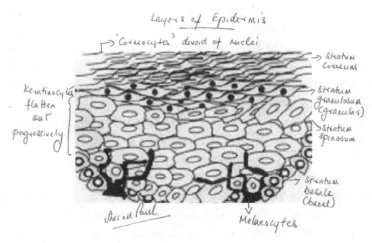

FIGURE 15   **Layers of epidermis showing progressive flattening out of cells**

In humans, parakeratosis is not found in hair-bearing skin, unless the patient is suffering from a disease like psoriasis. However, parakeratosis is normal in moist mucosal tissues, like that of the oral cavity or genital region. Therefore, when whales returned to water, their skin adapted to a moist marine environment, just as human tissues adapt to cope with the wet areas of the body, like the mouth or the vagina. Parakeratosis makes the upper layer of the whale's epidermis rich in phospholipids, thereby waterproofing the mammal.

Whale dermis also changed to adapt to marine life. The boundary between the dermis and epidermis can be an area of mechanical weakness when exposed to shearing forces. Finger-like formations, like dermal papillae, serve to strengthen the epidermis–dermis junction; and these are pronounced in whales. The more deep-diving the whale species, the more these inter-digitations are transversely orientated. As we look deeper in the dermis, we note that whale skin *lacks* hair, sweat and sebaceous glands.

Back in the cosy Reykjavik steakhouse, I began to feel guilty about being the one armed with a steak knife and rancid butter. My whale pepper steak arrived with a large bowl of fries. *Whale and fries?* The combination was both uncouth and delicious.

The next day, I visited the home of one of Iceland's great shark-hunters. All his ancestors had been shark-hunters. I watched as he hauled a trailer carrying a 1,000-kg Greenlandic shark. As I ran my hands over his latest catch, I couldn't help noticing how rough sharkskin is. Like coarse sandpaper.

The body fluids of most sea creatures are at a lower concentration than seawater. As a result, they must drink a lot of water or lose electrolytes by osmosis. Among sharks, however, the concentration of salts in their bodily fluids is *higher* than in seawater. Therefore, they don't drink much water and tend to have high concentrations of waste products like urea in their blood. As urea is toxic, their blood contains trimethylamine oxide, which neutralizes the damage caused by urea. However, the Greenlandic shark has no kidneys, and so the skin serves as its excretory organ. This skin, laden as it is with urea, is toxic if ingested. Urea makes sharkskin smell of urine, and hence gave rise to the Inuit legend of Skalugsuak.

The story goes that, a very long time ago, an old woman was washing her hair and body in urine (urine-bathing was practised in ancient times, especially in cold climates, due to the lack of hot water). She was using a washcloth and suddenly a massive gust of wind blew the cloth away. The woman watched helplessly as the washcloth landed a distance away, in the middle of the Arctic Sea. However, as she watched in amazement, her cloth, the Inuit say, became 'skalugsuak', the Greenlandic shark. This was the explanation the Inuit had for the unusual smell that emanated from the skin of these giant lethargic sharks.

So languid is the Greenlandic shark that, in spite of its impressive breadth and weight—it's over 20 feet long and weighs over a tonne—the hungry Inuit would be able to lure it towards a hole in the ice and grab it with their bare hands. From this arises their reputation as providers. Closer to modern times, descendants of the Vikings, like the Icelanders, were more likely to have used harpoons. However, in the process of discovering that the Greenlandic sharks lack kidneys and therefore have toxic skin, a few brave Icelandic lives would have been sacrificed. Nowadays the shark is buried under the ground, and the soil does its thing to detoxify that poisonous skin. Soil bacteria possess urease, an enzyme that catalyses the conversion of the urea molecule to two ammonia molecules and one carbon dioxide molecule.

$$(NH_2)^2CO + H_2O \rightarrow CO_2 + 2NH_3$$

The protein urease was first discovered in the 1920s. It is produced by many bacteria, yeasts and several plants, which explains its presence in soil. Some human bacteria also produce urease, a fact that is significant in medical practice. For example, *Helicobacter pylori*, implicated in the production of stomach ulcers, produce urease. A rapid urease test is therefore used in clinical practice as a diagnostic tool to detect the presence of this bacterium.

As the sharkskin putrefies, the soil urease converts the urea into ammonia. After six weeks, the shark is dug up, cut into strips and hung to dry in the Arctic freeze (see the *plate section* for an image of what that looks like). It is eaten after six months.

Opinions are divided in Iceland as to the name of this national dish, *hákarl*—should it be called putrid shark, smelly shark or rotting shark? It is reputed to be a longevity-enhancer. 'When in Rome ...' I decided. The putrid Icelandic shark was surprisingly tasteless. Maybe I couldn't smell it because we were all washing it down with *brennivin*, the local spirit named 'black death' due to its greater than 40 per cent alcohol content. We proposed a toast to the shark hunter. *Skál*, I said, raising my glass. Cheers. A Finnish blonde smiled at me and said, *kippis*.

The shark hunter then took me to his family chapel, which was located in the grounds of the shark-processing facility where we had been sampling hákarl. All his ancestors had been buried in the yard of this small church, and inside hung a painting of Jesus and his disciples. His family's legend had it that a famous Dutchman was shipwrecked, then saved by one of his ancestors whilst they were hunting sharks. The Dutchman returned with a painting by a famous Dutch artist, and that now hangs on the altar of the family chapel. The old shark hunter closed the windows of the church and asked me to walk past the painting, from left to right. When I followed his instruction, Jesus' eyes in the painting moved from side to side, following me. I retraced my steps to make sure I was not imagining it. The eyes didn't let up. He did not allow me to take photographs for fear that the painting would be damaged, or this illusory effect diminished. He asked me what I was doing in Iceland, and then whether being a skin cancer surgeon was my hobby, or writing was my hobby. 'Writing,' I said, 'although I'm never sure.' He wrote down something for me on a piece of paper. It said: *Blindur er bóklaus maður*.

Back at the hotel, I asked the bookish receptionist to translate the words on that scrap of paper for me. '*Blind is a man without a book*; it is a very old Icelandic proverb,' she said.

I had by now become good friends with Helge, a Norwegian plastic surgeon and a prominent figure in the Norwegian Aesthetic Surgery Society. Helge and I had spent some time relaxing in the Blue Lagoon, famed for its healing properties. There are silica rocks on the sides of the lagoon and everyone uses the silica as an ointment for the skin. I applied some to my face and soon it looked like a beetroot. I worried that it might be permanent. What would my patients think? I always tell them to test for allergies by applying a test dose of any new cosmetic cream behind their ears or on their arms!

I remembered that Reykjavik was the seat of the famous 'chess match of the century' between Bobby Fischer and Boris Spassky. Indeed, the spirit of chess still endures; I saw a few chess players in the town square as soon as I arrived in Reykjavik.

Bobby Fischer, towards the end of his life, became reclusive, neurotic, paranoid and 'stateless', and Iceland had offered him residence after the US refused to allow him entry post a trip to Japan. In his prime, Fischer had been obsessive about chess and had admired Marcel Duchamp, a French artist who gave up art for chess. Duchamp had described an opening called trebuchet or 'the trap'. But his favourite chess position was of an endgame called the Lasker–Reichelm position: a rare and unique position where black cannot win, but at best delay events. Did Bobby Fischer feel his life had become like the Lasker–Reichelm position, I wondered—much like the last fin whale entering Icelandic waters. Fischer knew that *his* deadly endgame had begun. There is a story that when he landed in Iceland, Fischer complained to his friend, Einar Einarsson, that there were no park benches. It is said that Einar showed him a volcanic rock to sit on instead. Since Fischer's death in 2008, that rock has a sign that says: 'Bobby's Bench', with an Icelandic proverb below it that translates thus: *Twice is the one relieved who sits himself on a stone.*

As I sat on Bobby's Bench alone, jotting down notes from my trip to Iceland, I spied some kids carrying fish they'd caught—

sticklebacks, the sort of fish kids can catch easily, as they are found in shallow water and estuaries. Sticklebacks are another classic example of skin evolution and adaptation. When the Ice Age ended, the giant glaciers melted and created many lakes and estuaries in northern Europe and America. The marine ancestors of the Icelandic sticklebacks were forced to undergo dramatic evolutionary change. These isolated populations of fish adapted to new freshwater sources, predators, water colour and temperature. They especially changed their skin colour to camouflage themselves in fresh water and to attract new mates.

David Kingsley, of the Stanford University School of Medicine, studied the genetic basis for this change in skin pigmentation of various stickleback species across the world. He and his colleagues crossed several species that had differences in skin and gill pigmentation, whilst searching for chromosome segments in the offspring that were always associated with inheritance of dark or light gills and skin. Through detailed mapping of one such segment, Kingsley and his colleagues found a gene associated with the inheritance of skin pigmentation—it's called KITLG, or KIT ligand.[2]

Later, they would discover that KITLG seems to have a greater role in the grand scheme of skin pigment evolution than originally thought. It is common scientific knowledge that humans originated 'out of Africa' about 100,000 years ago. As these ancient humans migrated into northern and colder climates, they no longer needed dark skin to protect themselves against the intense African sun.

David Kingsley and his colleagues noted that humans also have a KITLG gene, and discussed its significance in regulating the pigmentation of human skin, i.e., making our skin lighter or darker. It is now known that humans with two copies of the African form of the KITLG gene have darker skin colour, when compared to people with one or two copies of the new KITLG variant that is common in Europe. Interestingly, lightly coloured fish also have regulatory mutations that reduce expression of the KITLG gene in gills and skin.

This makes the KITLG gene one of the key regulators of skin colour adaptation in both fish and humans. This is the real beauty of the evolution of skin. The change in colour is regulated by the *same* gene in *different* animals, from the lowly stickleback to all-conquering humans. Sticklebacks changed skin colour to adapt to freshwater colours and camouflage themselves; humans changed skin colour based on the need for sun protection and possibly also to attract mates, a sort of sexual selection process. This may seem controversial, but researchers have found that in each society, specific culturally learnt mating preferences actually led to the dominance of specific biological traits in the opposite sex. It may have been that, in Europe, lighter skin was considered more sexually attractive because darker skin was more prone to rickets (which caused skeletal deformities) in the areas of northern Europe where the sunshine hours were very low.

This isn't as far-fetched as it may seem. Darwin himself once remarked: 'The sight of a feather in a peacock's tail, whenever I gaze at it, makes me sick.' He was referring to the fact that this process of 'sexual selection' was all about aesthetic fitness, in contrast to his baby, 'natural selection', which was all about survival fitness.

Changes in skin colour are mediated by the same ancient genetic apparatus in both humans and fish, or peacocks for that matter. Does this not sound similar to our discussion earlier about the role of cadherins in ancient sponges and skin cancers, and how cadherins are found in both primitive organisms and human beings?

Nicole King, the American biologist whose work with choanoflagellates we discussed, says: 'This is consistent with the idea of evolution as a tinkerer, cobbling together tools that are already available, rather than inventing a new widget.'

NOTES

1. Charles R. Bennett, in his review of *Island Life: A Natural History of the Islands of the World* by Sherwin Carlquist, published for the American Museum of Natural History [by] the Natural History Press, 1965.

2. Chemically speaking, a ligand is a molecule that binds with a central metal atom; kit ligand is a gene which acts as a stem cell factor.

FIVE

A Tale of Two Vitamins

The Earth has a skin and that skin has diseases, one of its diseases is called man.

– Friedrich Nietzsche, German philosopher and scholar[1]

The colour of the face differs much more widely in the various kinds of monkeys than it does in the races of man; and we have some reason to believe that the red, blue, orange, almost white and black tints of their skin, even when common to both sexes, as well as the bright colours of their fur, and the ornamental tufts about the head, have all been acquired through sexual selection. As the order of development during growth generally indicates the order in which the characters of a species have been developed and modified during previous generations; and as the newly born infants of the various races of man do not differ nearly as much in colour as do the adults, although their bodies are as completely destitute of hair, we have some slight evidence that the tints of the different races were acquired at a period subsequent to the removal of the hair, which must have occurred at a very early period in the history of man.

– Charles Darwin[2]

HUMAN MIGRATION AND THE CHANGES IN SKIN COLOUR

The study of skin anthropology is one of the areas where the tyranny of the prejudiced, the challenged and the inefficient is obsolete. As an organ, skin is both unique and diverse. Any other organ can hide mediocrity behind layers of, well, skin. If a liver or a kidney is not up to the mark, you may never know unless you were to take a medical test or examination. Skin wears its health like a badge for all to see—everything is unashamedly laid bare. Here it is, an organ that once developed disparate competing colours to help rebuild a species, and in doing so, displays this simple fact: evolution and skin colour are not words we visit in a book or museum; they are windows to the soul of our natural origins.

Anthropologist Nina Jablonski is considered one of the foremost experts on skin evolution. Several years ago, at the University of Western Australia, she was dismayed to find that many existing theories on skin, especially skin colour, tended to be racially biased. For example, many scientists suggested that white skin was more resistant to cold weather, although groups like the Inuit are both dark and well adjusted to cold climes.

Humans and their closest living relatives, chimpanzees, were separated from their common ancestor around six million years ago, with each strain developing into different branches. This common ancestor was covered with dark hair, and had light skin underneath. Around four million years later, or two million years ago, *Homo erectus* migrated out of Africa.

By now, this ancestor had a larger brain and more developed hand skills. This, in turn, brought with it certain problems. The body had to work harder to keep the brain cool (just as a computer needs a cooling fan) as physical activity and the use of hand tools increased. Although *Homo erectus* was not the first hominid to walk upright, he walked faster and migrated further, which also required cooling. To cool, he needed to sweat. To sweat properly, he required many sweat glands and a naked body. Figure 16 shows areas where people 'out of

Africa' still exist. And these aboriginal people—such as indigenous Australians or the negritos who inhabit the Andaman Islands in India or the Philippines—have particularly high concentrations of sweat glands when compared to more 'recent' (from an evolutionary point of view) migrants.

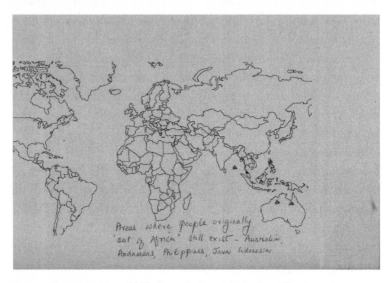

FIGURE 16   'Out of Africa' populations exist in places like Australia and the Andamans even today

Apes like chimpanzees have dark black hair but light pinkish skin. As man evolved from apes, he lost the thick hair and emerged rather naked. This evolution into a 'naked ape' necessitated a darkening of the epidermis of the skin to protect against sun UV damage. However, when we mention the worst effects of UV damage, one thinks of skin cancers such as malignant melanomas, or wrinkling and signs of ageing. But from an evolutionary point of view, changes occur to preserve the species—individual reproductive success is what becomes most important. Issues like cancer or beauty are not as important from an evolutionary point of view; in all its wisdom, nature knows that beauty doesn't last, but a species has to. The explanation for the darkening of skin is that the sun causes photolysis of folic acid (folate), a metabolite essential for normal neural tube function. Therefore, to preserve folic acid, and thereby the species' reproductive ability, African skin *evolved* to become dark. Once humans evolved into a state of nakedness, the pinkish skin of apes blackened to preserve folic acid.

When early Africans moved to northern Europe and places like Iceland, their skin became more transparent to sunlight, enabling those humans to produce sufficient amounts of Vitamin D, given the low annual sunshine hours.

It is no coincidence that neural tube defects, such as spina bifida and anencephaly, are far less common in the tropics than in the more temperate climates. It is also no coincidence that countries in Asia and Africa have larger populations when compared to Western countries, even given poorer living standards and less health care available to help during pregnancy. In India, when I graduated from medical school 25 years ago, medical doctors were not trained to routinely advocate folic acid for women planning to conceive, whereas it was routine in Western countries, given the higher risk of neural tube defects.

If you think about it, the only organ whose absence may threaten the biological existence of an animal on earth is the skin. No other organ or appendage is indispensable in quite the same way. Most animals, or plants for that matter, would shudder at the thought of a skinless existence. Perhaps this is why skin has always been very high on human consciousness, even venerated in ancient legends.

The Navajo tribe of American Indians, for instance, speak of 'skin-walking'. A witch or supernatural person was considered able to assume the identity of an animal by wearing the skin of that animal. So, a 'skin-walker' who walks naked, clad only in the animal fur of a coyote, becomes a coyote, or rather a werewolf-like hybrid creature. There was a ghoulish belief that these people first became evil skin-walkers by killing a member of their own families. Because the aspiring skin-walker needed to wear the pelt or skin of the animal whose characteristics he wanted to assume, removing the pelts of animals such as bears, coyotes, wolves and cougars are a strict taboo among the Navajo people. Sheepskin and buckskin are probably about the only hides used by Navajos, and the latter is reserved for ceremonies.

While conducting research on Navajo reservation, folklorist Barre Toelken heard stories about skin-walkers—in some cases, using a combination of skins to become (for example) part-dog and part-cat, while retaining the most vicious characteristics of both animals. In one instance, a Navajo police officer reported seeing 'four human figures, each with the head of a dog' after he pulled a speeding vehicle over and shone a flashlight through the driver's window. The legend of shape-shifters in Hollywood movies featuring American Indians is, in fact, derived from these skin-walkers.

Most other organs, like the heart or kidneys, didn't really have much to do with the early evolution of primitive creatures; *unlike* skin. For example, Greenlandic sharks don't have kidneys and starfish don't have hearts, but they *do* have skin. This is a fundamental fact. I suppose you could say that skin simply took on the responsibility of making things happen, sometimes adapting easily, at other times unwilling to change until it found a good enough reason to do so.

How does increased melanin production protect against UV damage? As a general rule, for solar radiation to produce biochemical damage, it needs to be absorbed. Melanin acts as an optical and chemical filter that reduces penetration of all UV wavelengths into sub-epidermal tissues. As an optical filter, it works through a scattering effect. The low levels of folic acid deficiency in Africa, even when nutrition is relatively poor, points to the highly melanized skin protecting against UV-induced damage of folic acid.

As the first modern humans or *Homo sapiens* migrated out of Africa into Europe 100,000 years ago, their skin lightened to allow more sun penetration to facilitate the production of Vitamin D. In colder polar climates, it was even more important to produce enough Vitamin D as the sun disappeared for long periods. It was important that the skin was light to best absorb Vitamin D when it was available. Natural selection may have played a part here. When dark-skinned people arrived in Europe, which had low levels of sunlight, many developed rickets due to deficiency of Vitamin D. Rickets cause not only skeletal problems and bone deformities, but also infertility. This was a double whammy—both from a sexual selection and a natural selection point of view. Deformed individuals were less likely to be 'chosen' and infertility ultimately 'bred' them out. Skin, therefore, lightened to enable enough Vitamin D production. There were good reasons for dark skin in Africa, but in European climes it just did not make sense. It was a battle between two vitamins, and skin ended up becoming the final arbiter.

In dark skin, Vitamin D exists in the form of Vitamin D3, a precursor to Vitamin D. However, when people with dark skin move to temperate climates, there is often not enough sun exposure to produce this pre-Vitamin D (Vitamin D3). This makes them prone to Vitamin D deficiency and diseases like rickets and osteoporosis. The increased melanin makes it more difficult for skin to absorb sunlight (when compared to white skin, which is 'native' to these climes). This initially puzzled me, because virtually all my patients of Indian or subcontinental descent are low in Vitamin D, even though there is plenty of sunlight in Australia and New Zealand. This is not only because the high UV index causes even more sun avoidance than in the tropics; I've seen many outdoor workers with low Vitamin D levels. This is because subcontinental skin is—from an evolutionary point of view—European skin that has become re-pigmented to *adapt* to the tropics.

Australia is interesting from a skin evolution point of view because of the high UV index, plentiful sunshine hours and a large Celtic population that wasn't 'designed' to live in such high-UV conditions. Furthermore, for several decades, Australia had an openly stated 'white Australia' immigration policy that encouraged people of European descent to migrate there preferentially over other races. In 1901, the Australian Immigration Restriction Act put this policy into effect; in 1966, the Harold Holt government began to dismantle it. 'White Australians' hadn't evolved to suit the land, which might explain why Australia has one of the highest incidences of skin cancer in the world.

The double-stranded structure of DNA is worth studying when we look at sun damage in skin. When skin is exposed to UV radiation, photons in the radiation cause damage to the DNA by altering its nucleic acid sequences into 'dimers'; i.e., it leads to the formation of A-T A-T dimers, rather than the usual A-T G-C sequence (*see Figure 17*). If these sequences are not repaired, the abnormal DNA divides abnormally, leading to production of skin cancer cells later on. Therefore, the body mobilizes certain enzymes to bring this sequence back to normal. In dark skin, with an abundance of melanin, not too many dimers are created (because the large melanosome shields the nucleus where the DNA is stored) and the bodily enzymes are more than capable of repairing the damage. In red-headed or Celtic white-skinned people, for example, due to the lack of a large melanosome sitting above and shielding the nucleus, the DNA sustains severe damage, i.e., several pairs of dimers are created. The body mobilizes enzymes, but the enzyme stores are often not enough to repair the damage properly, leading to a higher risk of skin cancer.

I often use diabetes as an analogy when teaching my students the DNA theory. Everyone is born with a supply of insulin in the pancreas. Some people are born with a genetic deficiency and this leads to type-1 diabetes in childhood; this is the rarer form and these people need insulin injections lifelong. Most people, however, develop type-2 diabetes because they have eaten too much over time, and this overindulgence makes them run out of insulin stores in middle age. Therefore, they need to take tablets that can increase insulin production or improve tissue uptake; some of these people end up on insulin injections. Type-2 diabetes is becoming all too

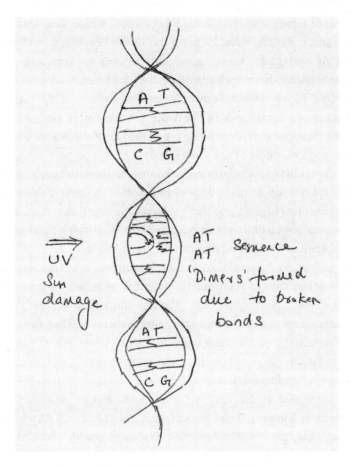

FIGURE 17   UV sun damage in DNA

common (with our fondness for carbohydrates and overeating) these days.

Some people are born with a deficiency of the enzymes that repair the damage that skin DNA sustains from UV radiation. This genetic deficiency is found in a condition called xeroderma pigmentosum. These people develop a multitude of skin cancers. White-skinned people *do* have these enzymes. But excessive exposure to the sun, or overuse of suntanning beds, or a severe sunburn damages the skin until repair systems can no longer cope, which then leads to skin cancer. In Queensland, after a day at the beach, it was almost a rite of passage for young teenagers to run a hot bath and peel skin off each other's backs because they had sustained blistering sunburns! No wonder then that Queensland has one of the highest incidences of melanoma in the world: of nearly 80 per 100,000 people. Fortunately, this practice is less prevalent these days due to increasing awareness of skin cancer risk.

In dark skin types, the large melanosomes sit above the nucleus and shield it from sun damage. This stimulation of melanin is therefore a defence mechanism against the sun. Amongst the Australian aboriginal population, which emerged out of Africa 65,000 years ago, there are virtually no skin cancers to be found.

However, as I mentioned earlier, evolution only considers as important matters of reproductive potential. Skin cancers generally occur in older age groups, when the reproductive peak is past—so evolution does not care about skin cancer mortality. Therefore, the best hope for a game-changing skin cancer treatment is genetic manipulation or 'prophylactic vaccine treatment', and not the passage of 'evolutionary time'.

I mentioned earlier that virtually all my Indian patients were deficient in Vitamin D. As ancient man walked across Africa and through Europe, his skin lightened. But as migration reached the Indian subcontinent and ventured further south in Asia to more tropical climates, it resulted in a 'second-coming' darkening of skin. Therefore, Indian subcontinental and Asian skin became darker after an initial period of lightening. However, this darkening of skin was an *adaptive* response to preserve folic acid (and ensure propagation of the species) under the tropical sun and not an *evolutionary* response.

To clarify further, modern human's migration out of Africa took thousands of years of evolutionary planning. Nature undertook this delicate task, sometimes forcing itself to brutally exterminate inferior species or useless organs. Every such assassination needed meticulous contrivance, and skin merely served as a well-briefed hitman. Therefore, African populations developed higher Vitamin D levels because, over time, they developed metabolic changes in their calcium metabolism. To confirm this evolutionary theory, Martine Luxwolda studied Vitamin D levels in African populations, especially in locations from where early man originated, and where the population was still on a traditional diet. Although she knew she would find high values, it was a surprise that they were quite so high. She says:

> Since nothing in biology makes sense except in the light of evolution, we decided that looking at traditional society would provide us with the Vitamin D status that was most likely present in humans when they adapted to their environment ...

Luxwolda and her team studied the 'traditional people' in Tanzania. They found that this population had 115 nmol per litre (nmol/l) of Vitamin D (more specifically, serum 25-hydroxyvitamin D) on an average, as compared to the 30–60 nmol/l that Westerners had.

Contrast this with my finding of low Vitamin D levels in virtually all my Indian patients. The Vitamin D deficiency in Indian subcontinental people is due to a combination of re-pigmentation of skin that had to adapt to the tropical sun, a vegetarian, cereal-based diet and avoidance of sun to prevent darkening of skin by tanning (which could lead to reduction in social status). Further, unleavened breads like chapatti have been shown to bind to calcium, further interfering with calcium metabolism. It has long been known that fish oils are a rich source of Vitamin D. It is interesting that Bengali brahmins eat fish, which they consider 'vegetable from the sea' (ancient wisdom rooted in science perhaps).

In the final analysis, the emergence of different skin colours was essentially a battle between two vitamins—folic acid and Vitamin D. And while the original dark colour of skin in Africa was evolutionary—to preserve folic acid—once early humans had lost much of their bodily hair, the other dark skin colours that came into existence were adaptive, depending on their environment.

Hairy animals like dogs, which lack skin sweat glands, develop mechanisms to lose bodily heat, including increased blood flow to hairless external ear canals (relatively hairless when compared to bodily fur), cooling of blood in the veins by evaporation of water from nasal passages and sinuses, and last but not least, by shallow rapid inhalations (as I am writing this chapter, my bored dog, Zack, is panting in my ear, having just eaten my last illustration in an attempt to woo me away from my desk).

Around 2.4 million years ago, a new type of hominid, *Homo erectus* appeared in East Africa. The tropical climate of the open African savannah is completely different from that of a humid rainforest. The ground temperature remains high at around 30^0C, and the animal (or human) is exposed to direct sunlight as well as reflected sunlight radiating from other objects. This new member of the hominidae family, i.e., the early human, adapted by losing bodily fur and developing sweat glands that cooled the body by evaporation. Walking on two legs also helped to cool the brain by draining some of the venous blood away from the head.

Morgan, in her book *The Aquatic Ape: A Theory of Human Evolution*, claimed that walking in a bipedal position, as opposed to the quadrupedal position of earlier apes, reduced direct solar radiation. Morgan's theories have been disputed by experts on the grounds that maintaining an upright posture needs more work and therefore generates more heat—this more than compensates for any gain. (For example, if we walked in a desert for a day, it is estimated that we'd lose more than eight litres of water.) It is, therefore, more likely that bipedalism happened as man developed more tools and began to use forelimbs more effectively for tasks, rather than to reduce solar radiation. However, walking upright would have helped cool the brain somewhat.

Comparative physiologist Knut Schmidt-Nielsen has suggested that change in air temperature induces changes in the smooth muscles of facial blood vessels. Venous blood drains from the face down the ophthalmic veins and their tributaries, allowing arterial blood to cool in the cavernous sinuses, before proceeding to supply the brain. Extending this theory, Fialkowski has suggested that brain size also increased to prevent overheating. As an adaptive response to the increased physical activity of hunting–gathering and endurance-hunting, hundreds of new neuronal connections developed in the brain to allow some to always be in working order. In other words, he suggests that we always have some spare 'cool' neuronal circuits. However, I doubt this theory—of the brain increasing its size due to temperature changes—stacks up, and many experts have dismissed it.

Quoting Charles Darwin again, in *The Descent of Man*:[3]

> Of all the differences between the races of man, the colour of the skin is the most conspicuous and one of the best marked. It was formerly thought that differences of this kind could be accounted for by long exposure to different climates; but Pallas first shewed that this is not tenable, and he has since been followed by almost all anthropologists. This view has been rejected chiefly because the distribution of the variously coloured races, most of whom have long inhabited their present homes, does not coincide with corresponding differences of climate.

Some people challenge the theory that human skin lightened to allow greater production of Vitamin D because people who live at the Arctic Circle, like the Inuit, have dark skin. However, the counter to this is the theory that, like polar bears, the Inuit have a diet rich in Vitamin D from salmon and fish oils and therefore did not need to produce Vitamin D by lightening their skin as an adaptive response. The Inuits, as I've often said in lectures, are virtually 'human polar bears'.

The last Ice Age, 80,000 years ago, caused large parts of the Northern Hemisphere and the southern part of the Southern Hemisphere to be covered with ice. Because the ice was stacked up in great heaps on the land, the sea level was about 80 m lower than it is nowadays, and this caused the continental plateaus to rise above the sea level. At that time (between 80,000 and 100,000 years ago), people could actually walk overland via the Arabian peninsula, India, Indonesia and New Guinea through narrow straits to reach Australia. My illustration (Figure 18) shows this migration pattern.

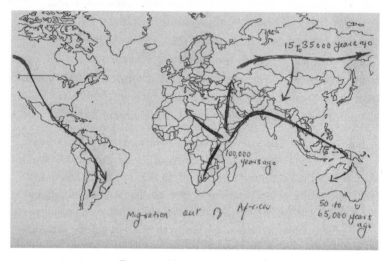

FIGURE 18 Migration out of Africa

So, while hominids appeared 2.4 million years ago, descendants of modern man left Africa only 100,000 years ago. However, evolutionary responses take much longer than that. This is why Darwin did not observe changes in the skin colour of Dutch families in Africa in three generations. Or why African people in Luxwolda's study had higher Vitamin D levels than Europeans even though they did not avoid sun or stay indoors like modern Asians. The evolutionary clock runs much slower than that.

In the end, this story should really be called the 'A Tale of Two Vitamins'—and that chronicle would summarize the evolution of different skin colours amongst human beings. When nature selected these two vitamins to do battle, it perhaps forgot to reconcile with ignorant human minds, which then began to question whether one colour was better than another, or if one was 'born to rule'.

For skin, any evolutionary call was a duty; when the order came to propagate a species, it responded. For me, the real beauty of its reaction is manifested in the many different skin colours around us. Swami Vivekananda, who not only helped take modern Hinduism to the West, but whose interest in science helped set up the Indian Institute of Science, once said:[4]

> All differences in this world are of degree, and not of kind, because oneness is the secret of everything.

Nature would agree, if only for the reason that it doesn't have the luxury of being able to go back and do things differently.

Notes

1. Dr Oscar Levy (ed.), *The Complete Works of Friedrich Nietzsche: The First Complete and Authorised English Translation*, Vol. 10, 'The Joyful Wisdom' (*La Gaya Scienza*), The Macmillan Company, New York, 1924.

2. Charles Darwin, 'Colour of the Skin', in *The Descent of Man*, D. Appleton and Company, 1871.

3. Charles Darwin, 'On the Formation of the Races of Man', in *The Descent of Man*, Appleton & Co., 1874, p. 167.

4. Los Angeles Review of Books. 'The Complete Works of Swami Vivekananda', http://lareviewofbooks.org/author.php?id=806, accessed 17 March 2012.

SIX

True Colours

By convention there is colour, by convention sweetness, by convention bitterness, but in reality there are atoms and space.

– Democritus, Greek philosopher (460–370 BC)[1]

Skin has no time to worry about beauty. It is busy with important tasks, like making sure it cocoons the body securely. Brooding and contemplation simply don't get tasks done.

The expression 'beauty is only skin-deep' is derived from a sixteenth-century poem praising the qualities of the ideal wife:

... And all the carnall Beauty of my Wife,
Is but skin-deepe, but to two senses knowne
~Sir Thomas Overbury (poem titled 'His Wife')[2]

The 'wife' referred to was not his. But the death that resulted from these words was his own.

Sir Thomas was infatuated with Robert Carr, who was a personal favourite of King James I. When Robert Carr, Earl of Somerset, met and came to be engaged to Frances Howard, Countess of Essex, an unhappy Sir Thomas wrote the poem 'His Wife' to his friend. On hearing about the poem from her fiancé—that his friend considered her beauty only 'skin-deep'—the Countess was enraged. So affronted was she that she plotted a rather elaborate and complex revenge.

As part of this scheme, the King appointed Sir Thomas as the ambassador to Muscovy, knowing he'd refuse. Upon refusal, Sir Thomas was arrested for insolence and committed to the Tower.

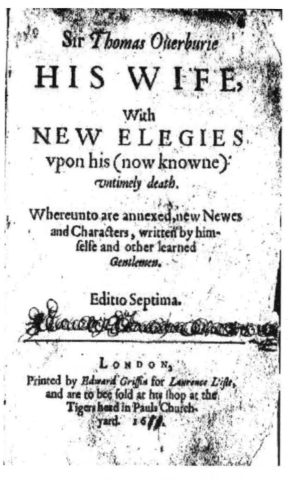

FIGURE 19   A posthumous edition of Sir Thomas
Overbury's poems[3]

The perpetrators then tried various poisons to eliminate him, including poisoning some tarts with mercury sublimate. Lord Somerset even sent his 'friend', Sir Thomas, a letter with which he sent him some white powder supposed to make his sickness better (it was actually arsenic). Sir Thomas Overbury's condition progressively worsened and he died, never suspecting this illness was not natural.

One of the reasons why skin colour is such an emotive subject in India is the complex connection between colour and caste. The word caste derives from the Portuguese 'casta', which means breed or lineage.

However, the modern Indian interpretation of lineage has unfortunately been only skin-deep.

In 1944, Brigadier Robert Eric Mortimer Wheeler (later Sir Robert) took charge of the Archaeological Survey of India and carried out extensive work at Harappa in the Indus Valley. He wrote:[4]

> The Aryan invasion of the Land of Seven Rivers, the Punjab and its environs, constantly assumes the form of an onslaught upon the walled cities of the aborigines. For these cities the term used in the Rigveda is pur, meaning a 'rampart', 'fort' or 'stronghold' ... Indra, the Aryan War god, is puramdara, 'fort-destroyer'.
>
> ...
>
> Where are—or were—these citadels? It has in the past been supposed that they were mythical, or were 'merely places of refuge against attack, ramparts of hardened earth with palisades and a ditch'. The recent excavation of Harappa may be thought to have changed the picture. Here we have a highly evolved civilization of essentially non-Aryan type, now known to have employed massive fortifications, and known also to have dominated the river-system of north-western India at a time not distant from the likely period of the earlier Aryan invasions of that region ...

Indian scholars of history have considerable debate on the events associated with the 'Aryan Invasion', with some disputing that it even happened; most agree that while there was some invasion, there was also some pre-existing civilization and Indian society evolved with the merger of these two peoples. Later on, scriptures like the *Manu Smriti* (c. 1500 BC), or the Laws of Manu, stated:[5]

> In this (work) the sacred law has been fully stated as well as the good and bad qualities of (human) actions and the immemorial rule of conduct (to be followed) by all the four castes (varna).

There are four varnas (literally, colours—'varna' in Sanskrit stands for both caste and colour) in the caste system. Scholars argue about whether, originally, each caste was denoted by a colour.[6] The brahmin priests were classified as having white skin. Below the priest were the kshatriyas or warriors, who were classified as being reddish in complexion. Below the warriors were the vaisyas or merchants, artisans and farmers, who were classified as yellowish; the labourers or shudras were classified as black. Lowest of all, outside the varna system, was the subculture called the 'untouchables', a caste distinction that sadly still exists in parts of India—and these people were considered too low to be even allocated a skin colour.

Manu's original description of varna may have come about because labourers toiling outside under the sun were more likely to have darker skin (adaptive response) than the brahmins, who probably spent most of their time indoors. Therefore, these skin colour changes were superficial and due to the environment. However, because arranged marriages tended to be within the same caste, eventually the gene pool became more and more whittled down, and the colour differences more visually discernible.

There is a scene in the American film *Outlaw of Gor*, based on John Norman's 'Gor' series of novels, in which the proprietor of an inn says, 'Money has no caste.' While wealth may nowadays overcome prejudice based on skin colour, Indian discomfiture regarding skin colour remains, and is captured in this poem, 'Skin',[7] by Reetika Vazirani, a very talented poet who migrated to the US, and then tragically killed herself and her two-year-old son in Maryland in 2003:

> even in this dark country
> we say Dasa darkone go to hell straight to
> we say varna color aura caste
> can't agree on codifications we sing
> lightskin light up my lucky sky
> fairskin fortune Bentley bright my Rolls
> look the apple-cheeked Kashmiri passes
> in a white club or look
> the darkness of the darkest member
> broad-nosed Dasa once a metropole's guard
> tee-time early to get him off the course first
> yet you're darker than he Krishna
> even a God can't explain what skin is
> sometimes I think Britishers hated
> their own pallor feared us I hid
> in my body macadam macabre …

We have already seen that, from a common origin, the KITLG gene orchestrated changes in skin colour in Asia—making us, scientifically and genetically speaking, from the same casta or lineage.

Sir Thomas Overbury found to his detriment that beauty was not skin-deep, but was only in the eyes of the beholder. And as far as the genetics of human pigmentation goes, differences between people or castes are *not even skin-deep*.

Richard A. Sturm of the Centre for Molecular and Cellular Biology at the University of Queensland, Brisbane (where I teach skin cancer surgery), has written an article titled 'Human pigmentation genetics: the difference is only skin deep', in which he discusses the role environment plays in the regulation of skin colour. According

COURTESY: AUCKLAND ZOO

Melur, the orangutan with dry palms

COURTESY: AUCKLAND ZOO

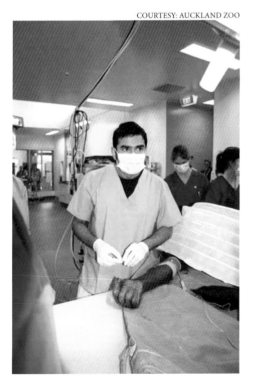

Melur and I, in surgery

Drosophila: one of the most studied organisms in biology and genetics

The French Flag model to help the understanding of how concentration levels impact the functioning of genes

High concentrations of a morphogen activate a blue gene	Lower concentrations of a morphogen activate a white gene	Red is the default state, i.e. below the concentration required to cause an activity

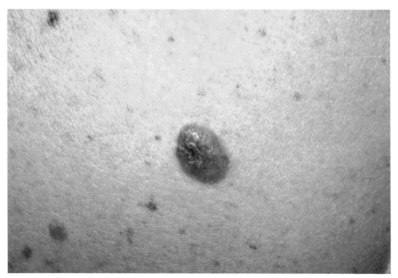

A typical basal cell cancer on the trunk in a patient with basal cell naevus syndrome

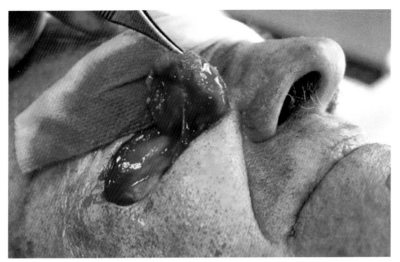

Defects in the cadherin–catenin circuits can lead to extremely invasive squamous cell cancers of the head and neck. I had to operate on this tumour recently; the tumour was extremely invasive around the eye and I had to use fairly complex cutaneous flaps to reconstruct the defect after removal of the tumour

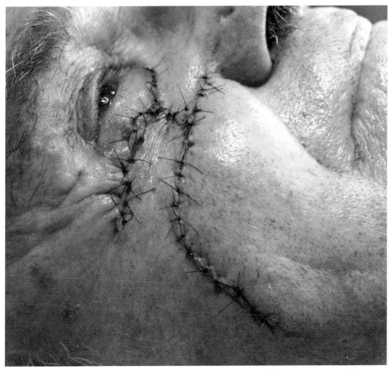

I have reconstructed the eye region using complex cutaneous flaps after surgically removing this aggressive squamous cell cancer

Giant Greenlandic sharks on a trailer

Shark skin drying after it has been de-toxified by soil in Iceland

The shark hunter
outside his family
chapel in Iceland

Sculpture from an Egyptian tomb of a couple who lived in the
time of the great pyramid builder, c. 2500 BC

The Von Luschan Chromatic Scale

Bauhaus optical
colour top

The Atwater Calorimeter

Kungsbrohuset Green building in Stockholm, powered by the body heat from commuters in the adjacent railway station

Reproduction of the painting 'Mikey' by John Bramblitt, who 'saw' by touch alone

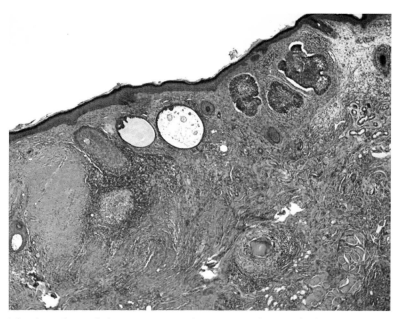

This histology slide specimen is from my archives of a biopsy showing a basal cell cancer

IMAGE COURTESY: LEECHLABS NZ

Medicinal leech

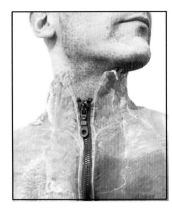

Oliver Goulet's SkinBag jacket

Another satisfied customer

to Sturm and others,[8] the first depiction of a range of skin colours in man dates back to around 1300 BC, and was found on the walls of the tomb of Sethos I. It showed a relatively fair-skinned Libyan and a very dark Nubian, together with an Asian and an Egyptian, who had skin tones between these two.

Frank Sweet, in his essay 'History of the US Color Line',[9] suggests that the earliest such depiction was much earlier, in 2613 BC when a statue portrayed Prince Rahotep and his consort Nefret of the Old Kingdom, early Fourth Dynasty. Many statues during the time of the great pyramid builders in Egypt depict interracial couples (*see plate section*).

These differences in skin colour have fascinated many researchers in recent history, even prompting some to develop charts to classify skin colour. One of the early charts, called the 'Luschan Chromatic Scale', was developed by Felix von Luschan. This was widely used in the early twentieth century, and abandoned in the 1950s.

It was a pretty crude method, especially because it resembled a paint palette catalogue—the sort you'd look through while choosing wall paint in a store. It consisted of 36 tiles which would be held against the untanned inner arm and a score registered. I've tried this myself, and found that you really cannot match human skin tone to a chart. Try matching your own skin colour to the original von Luschan chromatic scale (*see plate section* for a reproduction of the scale) and see how you get on.

Luschan was an interesting character, who after praising German military 'ironclads' and colonialism, was once quoted as saying:[10]

> The so called coloured peoples would promote mutual sympathy; racial barriers will never cease to exist, and if ever they should show a tendency to disappear, it will certainly be better to preserve than to obliterate them.

He was, however, a contradictory character who sometimes promoted racial purity and eugenics—he was once a member of the

German Society for Racial Hygiene, which espoused the principles of Aryan supremacy—and at other times repudiated anti-Semitism. So he did sometimes make statements sympathetic to the equality and understanding of races by saying:[11]

> Fair and dark races, long and short-headed, intelligent and primitive, all come from the same stock. Favourable circumstances and surroundings, especially a good environment, a favourable geographical position, trade and traffic, caused one group to advance more quickly than another, while some groups have remained in a very primitive state of development; but all are adapted to their surroundings, according to the survival of the fittest.

Native Americans are still often referred to as 'Red Indians'. At school, we were taught that this was because Columbus had originally thought he had discovered India, when he discovered the New World. Sure, but why 'red'? Von Luschan offers the following explanation:[12]

> From a mere scientific point of view … there is no more a yellow race, as there is a red one. We are accustomed to call redskins the American Indians but we know now, that they are not really red, but that the first Indians that had been brought to Europe had painted their skins red by mere chance; they might have just as well done this green or yellow … And so the races of Earlier Asia are not more yellow than the Italians or the inhabitants of Southern France.

Von Luschan would find a subject and typically test the inner arm, where the sun damage would not have caused much of a tan, because he was hoping to map the 'original' colour of a race or community. He'd run his cards along the skin until he found a match, upon which he would note down the corresponding number on his chart. If he was measuring a particular village or community, he would even calculate the average colour, which he called their 'mean shade'. The main problem with this method is that the matching of the colour to human skin is extremely subjective, and there is very little concordance between examiners.

Because the von Luschan chart proved so unreliable, people started using a Milton Bradley colour top. Milton Bradley is a US company that makes kindergarten supplies, and the colour top was originally a toy—a spinning top to teach kids about the merging of colours. It is a disc-like top that spins on a wooden spindle. By adjusting the combination of colours in the four discs, one could measure skin colour. This was first used in studying mixed-race people in Jamaica by Davenport. However, judgement had to be made with the tops rotating at full speed. Should the speed be reduced or vary, the recording became unreliable. Kerim Friedman, who teaches linguistic and ethnic anthropology in Taiwan, refers to a similar device, the Bauhaus *optischer farbmischer* (optical colour mixer) top, first designed by the Bauhaus artist Ludwig Hirschfeld-Mack. The principle is similar to the Milton Bradley colour top (*see plate section* for an image of the Bauhaus colour top).

Beatrice Blackwood published a paper titled, 'Racial Differences in Skin-Colour as Recorded by the Colour Top'.[13] In discussing the use of colour tops in assessing racial differences in skin colour, she wrote:

> The sampling and recording of skin tints in man is greatly facilitated by the use of a colour top, which enables us to record in percentage the proportion of black, red, white, and yellow discs required to make up the appropriate tint on its spinning surface.
>
> This method possesses the following advantages: It is capable of fine graduation, and hence, when certain precautions are observed, of greater accuracy than has hitherto been possible to the fieldworker. Records obtained with it can be treated statistically, and the results reproduced graphically or in colour for museum records or teaching purposes. The results obtained by different workers can be compared or used in conjunction if the personal equation is known. Experiment indicates that divergences between different observers amount to about +2 per cent for means of groups.

In practice, both the von Luschan charts and the colour tops were cumbersome and researchers therefore moved towards using spectrophotometers, which were more accurate and objective, as they essentially measured light reflected from the skin. In the early days, this was compared against a pure white standard, such as magnesium oxide, and nowadays against a calibrated standard of 100 per cent reflectance. I use fluorescence spectroscopy in my skin research, and while I don't use it specifically to measure skin colour, it is a serial and objective measure and much more accurate. As we've discussed earlier, it is the level of a single chemically inert and stable visual pigment, known as melanin, that is responsible for producing all shades of skin colours known to mankind.

If we look around supermarkets, we find that most of our breakfast cereals and fruit juices come fortified with many vitamins, including Vitamin C and Vitamin D. Nowadays we can also simply take Vitamin D supplements. Needless to say, in ancient Africa, in the absence of such technology, the skin had to absorb Vitamin D—abundantly available in sunlight-rich Africa. However, as we discussed earlier, sun causes photolysis of folic acid and, therefore, the skin had to have a certain amount of pre-Vitamin D (Vitamin D3) already present.

One of the discrepancies with the Vitamin D and folic acid theories I've discussed earlier is that we would then expect the Eskimos, like the Inuit, to be lighter-skinned than the Scandinavians, but they are darker-skinned. Similarly, Colombians would be expected to be as dark as Africans, but they are lighter-skinned. This is where diet may have played a part in the adaptive response. The Inuit diet is extremely rich in Vitamin D due to consumption of salmon and oily fish—cod liver oil, for example, has around 1,200 IU of Vitamin D per tablespoon, and salmon has around 300 IU per ounce. The European diet, in contrast, was cereal-based and so Vitamin D deficient. Over time, European skin had to adapt and become lighter, whereas Inuit skin did not. In Canada, where the Inuit are found in Arctic regions, health authorities recommend a daily dose of 400 IU, especially for women after age 50. If you compared that with the European diet, cereals (if unfortified) contain no Vitamin D and cheese only has around 4 IU per ounce.

In my skin clinic, I have noted that almost all patients of the Indian skin type seem to lack adequate Vitamin D levels. For instance, while breast-feeding is good for the baby, if the mother is Vitamin D deficient, it leads to the baby becoming deficient and can lead to serious problems. (Many infant formulae are actually fortified with Vitamin D.) In adults, Vitamin D deficiency can not only lead to brittle bones and teeth, but also affect general health.

In most patients, I advise short bursts of sun exposure. This is because there is a limit to the amount of Vitamin D that the skin can absorb, and spending all day in the sun has no significant benefit over two half-hour exposures.

We have noted earlier that Indian and Asian skin types are more prone to Vitamin D deficiency because of sun avoidance and dietary factors. However, the natural response of brown skin to the sun also increases the risk of Vitamin D deficiency. The Indian skin type responds to sun exposure by tanning. This is a protective mechanism, and also an immune response. We discussed earlier that the Indian skin type has a large melanosome in its cell, which positions itself directly above the nucleus and acts as a 'shade' for the nucleus of the cell, which is where all the genetic material is stored. While this protects brown and black skin types from genetic damage to the skin—and prevents dark-skinned individuals from getting skin cancers—this 'shading' also reduces penetration of solar radiation and therefore results in less production of Vitamin D.

Traditional wisdom was that calcium is the most important mineral for bone development, and women were advised calcium supplements. However, in clinical studies conducted on 72,000 nurses by Professor Willett at Harvard Medical School, it was shown that women with the highest intakes of Vitamin D (from food or supplements) had a 37 per cent lower risk of hip fracture than did the lowest consumers of Vitamin D. This study inferred that a high

Vitamin D intake was more important than high calcium intake for preventing hip fractures.

While the Harvard study was done on subjects with mostly white skin, it is even *more important* for people with dark skin to take Vitamin D supplements.

Vitamin D deficiency leads to calcium deficiency, and when we have low calcium levels, our bodies increase levels of two hormones—parathormone and calcitriol—that increase absorption of calcium from the intestines. This leads to more calcium inside our cells (intracellular calcium). High intracellular calcium levels lead to higher blood pressure and cellular fat. This finding—that low dietary calcium raises intracellular calcium—has been called the 'calcium paradox', and it has been suggested that it may also play a part in the development of arteriosclerosis, Alzheimer's disease, diabetes and muscular dystrophy. With a high vegetarian population and dark skin that avoids sunlight, India is now seeing an increase in heart disease and arterial disease, even in people who maintain otherwise healthy diets.

I recommend 1.25mg of Vitamin D (in the form of Vitamin D3 50,000 IU, or chole-calciferol) once a month for most of my patients. (Please check with your doctor if this regimen is suitable for you, as taking too much Vitamin D can lead to increased calcium levels, which can lead to kidney stones or heart irregularities. As with anything, too much of a good thing can be harmful.)

When people migrated out of Africa and moved to Europe, they also moved to a farm-based diet of cereals and dairy, and their dark skin was 'bred out' by natural selection. Because of their dark skin, these migrants from Africa could not produce Vitamin D and developed rickets. But those who migrated to regions *above the 55th parallel* could not farm grain, because it wasn't viable in those places. These people moved towards a diet of sea mammals and fish. On the other hand, in the same zone, where the Gulf Stream washes into the North and Baltic seas, it creates a 500-square-mile area around the Baltic where temperatures are surprisingly temperate, even given the Arctic dimness. Here, the people switched to farming and a cereal-based diet. Therefore, these people are extremely pale, in contrast to the darker Arctic folk living around them. Countries such as Latvia and Lithuania figure in this zone.

Back in New Zealand, on Fridays, I teach creative writing at disadvantaged primary schools. I always end up learning a lot while teaching these kids. We were discussing proverbs and sayings, and 'Beauty is only skin-deep' came up. Wanting to tell them what I had discovered about Sir Thomas Overbury, I asked the children if they knew where this proverb came from.

'From apples,' a young man piped up.

'Apples?'

'Beauty is only skin-deep. Apples look nice in different colours with skin on. Once you peel the skin, they all look the same and turn brown.'

This comment made me think about skin colour in apples. Of course, many hybrid species of apples have been artificially created, but what regulates colours in wild apples? Why are some apples green and others brown?

In most fruit, including apples, anthocyanins and chlorophylls are pigments that decide skin colour. If anthocyanin pigment accumulates, it results in the fruit becoming red; if chlorophyll predominates, the result is a green fruit. In apples, anthocyanin production is controlled by a distinct group of genes—the MYB transcription factors. If these genes are 'switched on', it leads to more anthocyanins being produced, making the fruit red. In humans, these MYB genes are linked to blood cell production. (The name 'MYB' originates from 'myeloblastosis'; 'myeloblasts' are primitive bone marrow cells from which blood cells are produced.) It is now known that sunlight is the 'switch' that turns on the MYB genes in plants. When apples grown in darkness were exposed to sunlight, MdMYB1 transcript (a type of MYB gene) levels increased over several days, correlating with higher anthocyanin synthesis, and turned the apples red.

It would therefore seem that the secret of skin colour changes in plants and humans is nothing but the genetic response to sunlight over time. All this biography has uncovered thus far is that, in the overpowering presence of the sun, skin has consistently balanced the pleasure of sensation with the sensibility of colour.

In 2004, writer Shelley Jackson began a unique project: to write a short story that had 2,095 words, she recruited 2,095 people from across the globe, each of whom would have one word of her story tattooed on his or her skin. Therefore, when the last of Jackson's 'words' dies, so too will her tale. Meanwhile, we may end up with an incomplete story, missing many words in the middle. Daniel H. Pink, covering this story for the *New York Times* magazine, wrote about this 'skin literature'.[14]

He wrote of how many participants were mainstream people, such as mothers and daughters who wanted words that were next to each other. Jackson also, apparently, encouraged 'her far-flung words' to get to know each other socially. Pink reports that she has heard from several dyslexics and librarians. On another note, in the FAQs on her website,[15] the author explains that participants can tattoo the word on any part of their body—unless the word names a body part. In that case, the participant can put it anywhere *except* that body part. There is, of course, one exception: the word 'skin'. That, incidentally, is also the title of Jackson's story. *Naturally.*

Notes

1.   Elizaberh M. Knowles (ed.), *The Oxford Dictionary of Quotations*, Oxford University Press, 1999, p. 257, accessed on 16 February 2013 at http://books.google.co.nz/books?id=o6rFno1ffQoC&q=colour#v=snippet&q=democritus&f=false.

2. Sir Thomas Overbury, *His Wife* (1622), English Poetry Full-Text Database © 1992 Chadwyck-HealeySource: Literature Online, http://gateway.proquest.com/openurl/openurl?ctx_ver=Z39.88-2003&xri:pqil:res_ver=0.2&res_id=xri:lion&rft_id=xri:lion:ft:po:Z200453421:2, accessed 17 March 2012.

3. Sir Thomas Ouerburie, *His Wife*, 1616, Image copy from: Harvard University Library.

4. R.E.M. Wheeler, *Harappan Chronology and the Rig Veda*, Cambridge University Press, 1947, p. 82.

5. *The Laws of Manu* 1500 BC, translated by G. Bühler, http://sanskrit documents.org/all_pdf/manusmriti.pdf , accessed 17 March 2012.

6. John Wilson, *Indian Caste* (originally serialized in *The Times of India*), William Blackwood & Sons, Bombay, Edinburgh and London, 1877.

7. Originally appeared as 'Radha to Krishna About Their Different Colored Skins'; in *Callaloo*, Triquarterly 109, Vol. 27, No. 2 (Spring 2004), p. 370.

8. K. Holubar, 'What is a Caucasian?', *Journal of Investigative Dermatology*, 106:800, 1996.

9. Frank W. Sweet, 'History of the US Color Line', in *Backintyme Essays: History of the US Color Line*, (wp 3.3.1), 21 May 2009, http://backintyme.com/essays/item/332, accessed 17 March 2012.

10. As quoted in John David Smith, 'W.E.B. Du Bois, Felix von Luschan, and racial reform at the fin de siècle', 2002, *European American Studies*, Vol. 47, No. 1, pp. 23–38.

11. Ibid.

12. Ibid.

13. Beatrice Blackwood, 'Racial Differences in Skin-Colour as Recorded by the Colour Top', *Journal of the Royal Anthropological Institute of Great Britain and Ireland*, Vol. 60, January–June 1930, pp. 137–68.

14. http://www.nytimes.com/2004/12/12/magazine/12SKIN.html

15. See www.ineradicablestain.com/skin-faqs.html

SEVEN

Mendel and Mouse Porn

Let it be borne in mind how infinitely complex and close-fitting are the mutual relations of all organic beings to each other and to their physical conditions of life. Can it, then, be thought improbable, seeing that variations useful to man have undoubtedly occurred, that other variations useful in some way to each being in the great and complex battle of life, should sometimes occur in the course of thousands of generations? If such do occur, can we doubt (remembering that many more individuals are born than can possibly survive) that individuals having any advantage, however slight, over others, would have the best chance of surviving and of procreating their kind? On the other hand, we may feel sure that any variation in the least degree injurious would be rigidly destroyed. This preservation of favourable variations and the rejection of injurious variations, I call Natural Selection.

~ Charles Darwin[1]

A number of scientific breakthroughs are the result of clear-eyed thinkers using simple inexpensive means to extract priceless information. The origin of skin colour, that skin colour was 'bred' by nature and circumstances, is an uncomfortable conversation to have. The idea that all skin colours just developed independently might be wrong, but it was socially convenient.

In the 2000 Republican Primary in South Carolina, a desperate attempt was made (deliberately or unwittingly) by the George W. Bush campaign to discredit Senator John McCain. A whispering campaign was allegedly organized, with telephone polls and posters asking, 'Would you vote for John McCain if you knew he had fathered a black child?' Republican strategist Karl Rove was considered the instigator of this vicious campaign. It was particularly distasteful because John McCain and his wife have an adopted daughter, Bridget, a dark-skinned child from Bangladesh with a cleft palate. She had been seen on the campaign trail with John McCain, and this made the smear both possible and plausible. As *Vanity Fair* reported in November 2004:[2]

'This whole thing, it was orchestrated by Rove, it was all Bush's deal ... It was pretty rank,' said [Roy] Fletcher [part of McCain's campaign management], 'and they had an institution that was peddling all that shit, and it was a university, Bob Jones University. I'm telling you, if there was a campaign headquarters in South Carolina, there it was.'

I quote this story to illustrate our prejudices and moral precepts when it comes to colour. Until this story came up, McCain had a sizeable lead, which this 'black child' campaign not only reversed, but transformed into an easy victory for Bush.

Colour bias is widespread in India even though most Westerners would consider Indians to be a mostly homogeneous populace. Anyone who knows India understands that the word 'fair' in India actually means 'fair-skinned'. *The Hindu*, a major Indian newspaper, reported on matrimonial advertisements in India:[3]

After being rejected, '100 billion times', [Sapna Sera Abraham, 32] informed her parents that she was tired of searching for the perfect partner. 'The mothers of the grooms are the ones who reject me immediately,' she says. 'For people like me who are so sensitive such rejections can be very hurtful. But I have reached a point where I do not care anymore.'

Let's say an alliance were to occur between a white woman and a black man, what are the chances of the child being completely black or white? If a father is half-black or half-white, what are the chances that a descendant would be completely black or white? Are such calculations the domain of mathematics or science?

Mathematician Marston Morse (1892–1977) once stated that mathematics is 'the sister as well as the servant of the arts'. Morse wrote in a letter to American educator, Dr Frank Aydelotte, in 1943:[4]

> I do not believe that the traditional influence of mathematics, its purpose, or its associations, are 'entirely different' from the influence, purposes or associations of the humanities … Mathematics is both an art and a science … In spirit we mathematicians at the Institute would cast our lot in with the humanists … Mathematicians are the freest and most fiercely individualistic of artists. They are subject to no limitations of materials or instruments. Their direction at any time is largely determined by their tastes and intellectual curiosity. Their studies are really the studies of the human mind. To me the work of Einstein is even more important as a free and beautiful expression of the creative imagination of an individual than as a part of the science of physics.

Nearly a century before Morse, a Moravian monk called Gregor Mendel began pottering around his garden in the 1860s. Mendel had studied mathematics, and to a mathematician, who viewed everything in the world as obfuscatory until proven by formulae, biology seemed too soft, almost like a pseudo-science. So he brought his mathematical methods to biology. Mendel's meticulous recording of the results of his experiments show mathematical precision and a spirit of scientific adventure—and, one may add, a certain impatience to have his questions answered.

The practical effect of Gregor Mendel's famous experiments with peas was the beginning of the study of genetics. I must note here that Mendel did not experiment with peas to begin with. His real obsession was the study of 'true' breeding and what would happen to mixed breeds. He was the first to wonder about the *inheritance* of skin colour in animals, especially mice: would albino mice bred with albino mice produce only albino offspring? What would happen if you bred an albino mouse with a 'mongrel' or part-albino mouse? He would have perhaps never got around to studying peas but for Bishop Schaffgotsch, who thought that it was unhealthy for a monk who had taken the vow of chastity to watch what amounted to mouse porn. Mendel is known to have remarked that he turned from animal breeding to plant breeding only because 'Bishop Schaffgotsch did not understand that plants also had sex'. Species rise and fall because of sex. What Mendel did was figure out a way to 'manufacture' species, so he could understand the inner mechanics of reproduction.

When Mendel's collection of fornicating mice was banished from the cold walls of the abbey, he sought refuge in the warm greenhouse and began to study peas. One of his missions was not only to breed hybrids, but to map with precision what happened when hybrids were bred with hybrids. He chose *Pisum sativum*, or peas, because they were easy to grow and produced two generations in a year. Nowadays, geneticists study faster breeders like the fruit fly, which reproduces within a fortnight after birth, or *Escherichia coli*, bacteria in the human colon that are often the cause of urinary tract infections, which reproduce every four hours.

It is worth taking a look at Mendel's early work to understand the brutal simplicity of his genius or why he is called the father of modern genetics. To explain this further, Mendel made an informed and inspired choice of subject—not only does a pea reproduce within six months, but the pea is an interesting being because it contains both male and female sex organs. Therefore, it is able to both 'self-pollinate' and 'cross-pollinate'. Mendel took 'pure-bred' yellow and green peas and cross-pollinated them to study hybrid behaviour. Figure 20 illustrates his early experiments.

When Mendel cross-pollinated yellow round peas with green angular ones (Mendel's terminology translates to 'angular'; English-

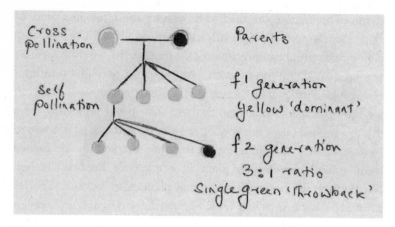

FIGURE 20   The inheritance of colour in peas
(in this image, yellow=light circles; green=dark circles)

speaking scientists agree that in this situation he really meant 'wrinkled'), he was astonished to find that in the first generation, every pea had preferentially inherited yellow and round traits: yellow had dominated green; round had dominated wrinkly. Mendel had discovered *dominant* and *recessive* traits—inheritance characteristics that we now call our 'genes'. Figure 20 shows yellow completely dominating green in the first generation. But in the following generation, a recessive green pea turned up as a 'throwback', in a ratio of 1:3. Gregor Mendel explained:[5]

> This is precisely the case with the pea hybrids. In the case of each of the seven crosses the hybrid-character resembled that of one of the parental forms so closely that the other either escapes observation completely or cannot be detected with certainty. This circumstance is of great importance in the determination and classification of the forms under which the offspring of the hybrids appear.
>
> Henceforth in this paper those characters which are transmitted entire, or almost unchanged in the hybridisation, and therefore in themselves constitute the characters of the hybrid, are termed the 'dominant', and those which become latent in the process 'recessive'. The expression 'recessive' has been chosen because the

characters thereby designated withdraw or entirely disappear in the hybrids, but nevertheless reappear unchanged in their progeny, as will be demonstrated later on.

Interestingly, as Mendel observed further generations, he was astounded to note that this 3:1 ratio persisted. Of course, as his experiments progressed down even more generations, he found the 3:1 ratios changed to 2:1:1 (*see Figure 21*), which he explained rather elegantly.[6]

The ratio of 3 to 1, in accordance with which the distribution of the dominant and recessive characters results in the first generation, resolves itself therefore in all experiments into the ratio of 2:1:1 if the dominant character be differentiated according to its significance as a hybrid character or a parental one. Since the members of the first generation spring directly from the seed of the hybrids, it is now clear that the hybrids form seeds having one or other of the two differentiating characters, and of these one-half develop again the hybrid form, while the other half yield plants which remain mutant

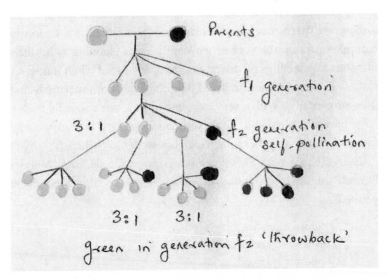

FIGURE 21   Mendel's peas—two generations down (in this image, yellow=light circles; green=dark circles)

and receive the dominant or recessive characters (respectively) in equal numbers.

Mendel established that each offspring inherited a particular trait from a parent. Each of these traits is a different 'gene'. There are *many* such independent individual traits that can be passed on; e.g., colour or shape characteristics. We now know this is possible because each individual trait is located on a different chromosome. Therefore, humans may inherit an eye colour trait from a parent, but that does not increase or decrease their risk of developing a funny-shaped ear that 'runs' in the family. Further, a trait may not show up in an individual but can still be passed on to the next generation as a 'throwback'.

Interestingly, although Mendel performed his research in the 1860s, his work was largely ignored until 1900, when William Bateson, a don at St John's College, Cambridge, embarked on a similar plant hybridization venture. When he read Gregor Mendel's paper, originally presented thirty-five years earlier, Bateson felt a chill down his spine. He was unsure if it was from shock or elation. This brilliant Austrian monk had already completely and meticulously compiled data on the very experiment he was planning as his life's mission. Any feelings of disappointment dissipated when Bateson's rather practical wife summarized the situation—both succinctly and unsentimentally: 'With a very long line to hoe, one suddenly finds a large part of it already done by someone else. One is unexpectedly free to get on with other jobs.' (Like house work, perhaps?)

Even if his work remained undiscovered for decades, Mendel himself foresaw the significance of his achievement in a poem he penned:[7]

> But unfading are the laurels of him
> Who earnestly and zealously strives
> To cultivate his mind
> Who with the full light of his understanding
> Seeks and finds the mysterious depths of knowledge,

Of him in whose development the germ
Of glorious discovery implants itself,
Nourishing him, and sending abundant blessing
To the thirsty crowd of mankind—
Yes, his laurels shall never fade,
Though time shall suck down by its vortex
Whole generations into the abyss,
Though naught but moss-grown fragments
Shall remain of the epoch
In which the genius appeared.

As Mendel began to widen the scope of his experiments beyond the humble pea on to brightly coloured flowers, he made the observation that colour in multicoloured organisms is determined by more than one gene or a combination of several different 'independent colour characters'. In the paper he presented in 1865, 'Experiments in Plant Hybridisation', which was translated by William Bateson, Mendel said:[8]

A white-flowered example of *Dianthus caryophyllus*, which itself was derived from a white-flowered variety, was shut up during its blooming period in a greenhouse; the numerous seeds obtained therefrom yielded plants entirely white-flowered like itself. A similar result was obtained from a subspecies, with red flowers somewhat flushed with violet, and one with flowers white, striped with red. Many others, on the other hand, which were similarly protected, yielded progeny which were more or less variously coloured and marked.

Whoever studies the colouration which results in ornamental plants from similar fertilisation can hardly escape the conviction that here also the development follows a definite law which possibly finds its expression in the combination of several independent colour characters.

There is an important skin colour gene called 'SLC24A5', which is a major factor in skin colour differences between populations in different continents.

The name SLC24A5 derives from 'solute carrier, family 24, member 5'. Solute carriers (SLC) are a group of membrane transport proteins that are made up of around 300 members organized into 51 families—the standard practice for gene nomenclature, which is how SLC24A5 got its name. SLC24A5 is essentially a 'transporter' (specialized proteins that facilitate transport of certain substances across cell membranes) that, in humans, is encoded by the corresponding SLC24A5 gene. While researchers are unsure how this actually regulates skin colour, it seems to have something to do with the movement of calcium into cells, leading to the theory that more calcium in the cell may mean more melanin.

In any case, the SLC24A5 gene comes in two variants, dark and light. People with two dark versions are black, and people with two light versions are white.

Let's look at the SLC24A5 gene as Mendel did with peas. Firstly, like peas in a pod, we share genes that denote skin colour. However, what makes us different is that, unlike a 'pure-bred' yellow pea in Mendel's experiment, we can share different versions of the gene. For instance, the SLC24A5 comes in dark and light variants. In Figure 22, I have called them D and L. If you inherit DD, i.e., two dark versions, your skin is very dark. If you inherit two light versions, your skin is very light. The thing to remember is that, like in Mendel's experiments with hybrids, if two DL parents (i.e., each with one dark and one light version) had offspring, it is possible for one to be a 'throwback' and inherit a DD or an LL. This means two lighter-skinned 'hybrid' parents could end up with a black child, or vice versa. Of course DL parents can have skin tones anywhere between black and white.

If you think about early human migration out of Africa, people with DD would have been more likely to develop rickets when compared to those with LL versions of the SLC24A5 gene. However, the DL folk, who were more in number, didn't fare too badly as they could

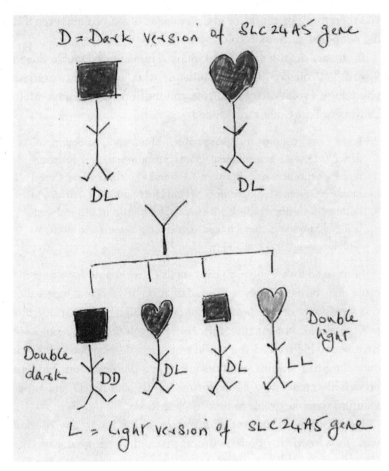

FIGURE 22 The passing on of the colour gene in
human beings

absorb more Vitamin D when compared to their DD counterparts. Over time, as diets became more cereal-based (further depleting Vitamin D), the DD or black skin types became extinct in Europe through the evolutionary forces of natural selection. Therefore, when man first ventured out of Africa, the SLC24A5 gene influenced skin colour development by breeding out the environmentally incompatible African skin type in European conditions. SLC24A5 was therefore a major factor in the *evolution* of skin colour, even if it did not per se cause skin colour change.

In an article titled 'Cereal Grains: Humanity's Double-Edged Sword',[9] Professor Loren Cordain, who researches exercise physiology, evolutionary medicine and nutrition at Colorado State University, Fort Collins, concluded:

> From an evolutionary perspective, humanity's adoption of agriculture, and hence cereal grain consumption, is a relatively recent phenomenon. ... between 5,500 and 10,000 years ago. Cereal grains represent a biologically novel food for mankind ... [lacking] a number of nutrients which are essential for human health and well-being; additionally they contain numerous vitamins and minerals with low biological availability.

Humans didn't 'evolve' to eat cereals or we would have become more like birds. However, the adaptation to a cereal-based diet was necessary for different reasons (we're talking grain, not fruits or vegetables). But for this 'agricultural revolution', we would not have been able to feed the world's burgeoning populations, given dwindling fish and livestock resources and deforestation. Modern processed cereals now come fortified with Vitamin D and other vitamins to make grains more complete foods.

Here I pose an interesting question: if the biography of skin was 'forwarded' to modern times, given that we now have the manufacturing ability to supplement Vitamin D and folic acid in our cereals and foods, would similar skin colour changes have evolved?

Remember I mentioned that I had seen sticklebacks during my trip to Iceland? Stickleback fish were originally dark-coloured when they were in the sea. As they migrated to rivers and estuaries and became freshwater fish, their skin tone lightened to blend in with their new surroundings, so they could avoid predators. Likewise, as Europeans migrated into Asia, their skin colour changed to become darker to adapt to equatorial conditions through the synthesis of more melanin. However, as they ventured further east, East Asians developed lighter skin to deal with colder climates. Scientists now know that skin colour in most lighter-skinned Asians is regulated by the KITLG gene, which researchers feel may also be involved in the change of hair colour from blonde to brown. A non-working KITLG gene causes East Asians to become lighter-skinned when compared to their South Asian counterparts. (Remember the French Flag model we discussed—even a non-working gene has an effect.) As in fish, the KITLG gene is the major factor in human skin colour change as an *adaptive* response to new environments.

To rewind a little, the entire range of human skin, hair and eye colours is regulated by a single inert pigment: melanin. As visible as these differences are, melanocytes make up only a small proportion of epidermal cells. These melanocytes are derived from precursor cells called melanoblasts, which arise from the neural crest (Figure 23). The neural crest develops from the neuroectoderm (which we discussed in Chapter 3, on gastrulation).

These melanoblasts then migrate to the epidermis, differentiate into more mature forms called melanocytes and then proceed to produce melanin pigments via the granule-like melanosomes. Eumelanosomes end up producing brown-black pigment called 'eumelanin', while pheomelanosomes produce red-yellow pigment called 'pheomelanin'. Pheomelanin produces red hair, while the eumelanin–pheomelanin combination produces a 'strawberry blonde'. Eumelanin is present in greater amounts in dark-skinned individuals, and is responsible for brown-black hair as well as darker skin tones. To truly understand how melanosomes produce different forms of melanin, one needs to understand this 'factory' at a biochemical level. John Jacob Abel once said:[10]

> As soon as we touch the complex processes that go on in a living thing, be it plant or animal, we are at once forced to use the methods of this science [chemistry]. No longer will the microscope, the kymograph, the scalpel avail for the complete solution of the problem. For the further analysis of these phenomena which are in flux and flow, the investigator must associate himself with those

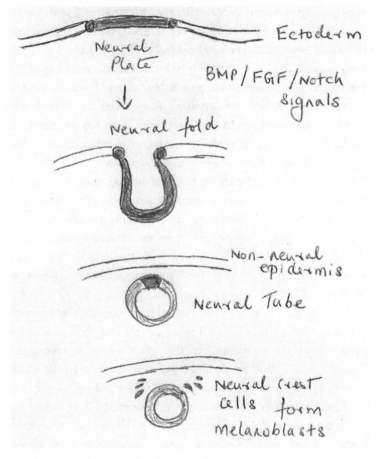

Ectoderm

Neural Plate

BMP / FGF / Notch Signals

Neural fold

Non-neural epidermis

Neural Tube

Neural crest cells form melanoblasts

FIGURE 23   **The development of neural crest cells**

who have labored in fields where molecules and atoms, rather than multicellular tissues or even unicellular organisms, are the units of study.

Take a look at Figure 24. Here, TYR is short for tyrosinase, an enzyme that is responsible for the first step in melanin production. A disruption in function of the TYR gene leads to an inherited pigmentary disorder—albinism.

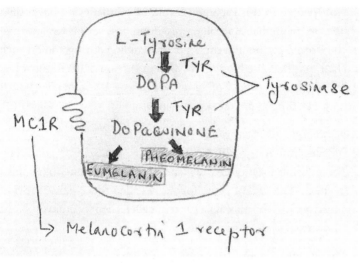

FIGURE 24   The function of tyrosinase

'Loss isn't science; it's a human reckoning,' Meghan O'Rourke said,[11] when discussing her book about loss, *The Long Goodbye*. But can we develop an understanding of science from loss, I ask myself. Isn't it best to study what happens when pigmentation is lost or defective, as a means of understanding the genetics of human pigmentation?

Kaposi was the first to study albinism. In 1985, he noted: 'Among the negro races (in whom, according to Beigel, a half-whitening of the dark colour, semialbinism, occurs) albinism is more frequent than in the light-coloured races.'[12]

The modern classification of the types of albinism is primarily based on *which mutated gene* causes disruption of melanin production in cells, rather than on outward physical signs. These gene mutations not only cause skin pigment loss but also corresponding changes in hair and iris colour.

Oculocutaneous albinism type 1:
❖ Gene mutation: TYR gene is considered responsible for OCA type 1.
❖ Location: chromosome 11.

Most people in this type are devoid of pigment and have milky white skin, white hair and blue eyes. Some less severe variants may produce some pigment in the form of freckling during adolescence, and hair may become blonde. A different version of TYR is involved in causing green instead of blue eyes, and yet another version in causing freckling in darker-skinned individuals.

Oculocutaneous albinism type 2:

❖ Gene mutation: OCA2 mutation genes are considered responsible for this (OCA2 is short for Oculocutaneous albinism type 2. The OCA2 gene, formerly called the P gene, provides instructions for making a protein called the P protein).[13]

❖ Location: chromosome 15.

This is more common among sub-Saharan Africans, African Americans and Native Americans than in other population groups. The hair may be auburn or red, eyes usually blue-grey and skin white. In Europeans, the condition is often difficult to detect because a person's skin just appears a bit whiter than the rest of the family. With exposure to the sun, this type of skin could develop naevi (moles) or freckles, making the diagnosis even more difficult. This could be why Kaposi felt the condition was more prevalent in Africa.

There is an interesting anthropological aspect to the OCA2 gene. Researchers now think that a mutation in an adjacent gene called HERC2 (the official name of which is 'HECT and RLD domain containing E3 ubiquitin protein ligase 2') may shut down the expression of the OCA2 gene. However, we already know that a non-working OCA2 gene is one of the steps needed for blue eyes. What this finding has shown scientifically is that *all* blue-eyed people have *one common ancestor*, and this person appeared as recently as 6,000 to 10,000 years ago.[14, 15] One working version of the OCA2 gene causes more pigment production and therefore eyes are brown rather than blue. By the way, another solute carrier gene, SLC24A4, determines green eyes rather than blue eyes. And a 'working' KITLG gene, which causes skin lightening, also causes hair to change from brown to blonde.

Oculocutaneous albinism type 3:

❖ Gene mutation: TYRP1 mutations cause OCA type 3 (TYRP 1 is short for Tyrosinase-related protein 1, which stabilizes tyrosinase).

❖ Location: chromosome 9.

This is a less common form of albinism and has been primarily identified in black South Africans. People with this disorder usually have ginger or reddish hair and hazel or brown eyes. It is also seen in New Guinea.

Oculocutaneous albinism type 4:

❖ Gene mutation: SLC45A2 gene mutation results in OCA4. (Remember we studied this particular solute carrier gene earlier in the formation of skin colour 'out of Africa'?)

❖ Location: chromosome 5.

This is also uncommon, although it is the most common form in East Asia. Type 4 and type 2 albinos are not easily distinguishable visually.

We have looked at TYR, so let's look at MC1R or Melanocortin-1-receptor gene, whose task it is to create a protein that turns pheomelanin (the red-yellow or light melanin) into eumelanin (the brown-black or dark melanin). Therefore, if you have a good working MC1R gene, you cannot have red hair because the pheomelanin has been converted into eumelanin. But if you have two copies of a defective MC1R gene (similar to having two L or light versions of SLC24A5), you end up with a build-up of pheomelanin—and red hair.

In 2007, *National Geographic* magazine caused a stir by suggesting that redheads were going extinct. This was reported in the *Daily Mail*, titled 'Redheads could be extinct in 100 years', and asking what William Shakespeare, Christopher Columbus, Prince Harry and Nicole Kidman had in common. *National Geographic* theorized, using the Vitamin D theory, that initially redheads (with two light versions of SLC24A5) had the advantage of absorbing more Vitamin D. The magazine suggested that as redheads only make up 2 per cent of the population, and as they are at higher risk of skin cancers, they wouldn't survive 'natural selection' or interbreeding. But as I said earlier, skin cancers aren't of much interest from an evolutionary point of view—given that most occur after an individual's reproductive peak.

However, this fear of extinction has also led to the popular fad of having certain days designated especially as a tribute to 'gingers'! The Edge radio station in New Zealand runs an annual 'Hug a Ginga' day (in 2012, it was on 25 May).[16]

My colleague Rick Sturm, researcher in hair and skin genetics at the University of Queensland, agrees that there will be no shortage of redheads in the world. About 40 per cent of Scotland carries the gene, and 13 per cent of Scots actually have red hair.

Red hair is caused by a mutation in the MC1R gene. The gene is also a recessive trait: if both parents are redheads, they pass on this mutated MC1R gene to their offspring. However, as we see from the Mendelian laws of inheritance, traits like red hair can skip a generation or two and resurface again, whatever hair colour the parents in intervening generations may have.

The poet Maya Angelou wrote a poem called 'Human Family':[17] 'The variety of our skin tones / can confuse, bemuse, delight'. She was right. Blacks were enslaved in southern USA, while albinos were ostracized in Nigeria, and a Facebook widget in India encouraged users to appear whiter.[18] Major human genes involved in the formation of melanin have now been identified using a comparative genomics approach, and through the molecular analysis of the pigmentary process that occurs within the melanocyte. We now know of many independent genes that regulate skin and eye colour, either by controlling melanocyte production or the type of melanin pigment produced by the cells. Biology has no bias, alas we humans do. As Adlai Stevenson once said in a speech:'Nature is neutral. Man has wrested from nature the power to make the world a desert or to make the deserts bloom. There is no evil in the atom; only in men's souls.'[19]

Now that we have gone over the science behind major genes that control skin and eye colour, I've got a quiz for you:

Quiz: You have to identify what gene or gene mutations likely caused the appearance given below. (Hint: all the answers are genes we have covered in this chapter.)

1. Typical Irish redhead with freckles and green eyes.
2. Maori woman in New Zealand with marked freckling of face.
3. Red hair and blue eyes.
4. Albino you came across in Melbourne, who hails from Korea.

The answers are at the end of this chapter, but do give it a shot![20]

How did you get on? Feel like taking up skin colour genetics as a hobby? Given that I travel a lot due to my teaching and speaking engagements, I amuse myself with this pastime when I am stuck at airports—looking at the parade of different skin colour genes and their hosts.

The strange thing is, all this chapter does is illustrate a certain commonality, a universal truth about skin colour. After all, how much real difference is there between humans, other than having a working or non-working variation of a gene? As a skin researcher, doctor and writer, I hope that my explanations of the human biology behind genes, vitamins and diet may help us understand our skin colours and that, taken at face value, they really denote nothing of value or superiority; what our skin colour gives us is a message, via a system of genes that seem to say this: skin colour is basically a sign on the road that leads us to the discovery of many genetic signals. If you remove these signs, all that is left is universal truism.

Notes

1.　Charles Darwin, *The Origin of Species*, Chapter 4: 'Natural Selection', http://www.talkorigins.org/faqs/origin/chapter4.html, accessed 17 March 2012.

2.　Richard Gooding, 'The Trashing of John McCain', *Vanity Fair*, November 2004, http://www.vanityfair.com/politics/features/2004/11/mccain200411, accessed 17 March 2012.

3.　Sowmiya Ashok, 'A life of slim chances and unfair expectations', *The Hindu*, 8 March 2012, http://www.thehindu.com/news/cities/chennai/article2971824.ece, accessed 17 March 2012.

4.　Marston Morse's letter quoted in Joanne E. Snow, 'Mathematician as Artist', *The Mathematical Intelligencer* 2010, Vol. 32, No. 2, pp. 11–18.

5.　Gregor Mendel, 'Experiments in Plant Hybridisation', translated by William Bateson, paper read at the Meetings of The Natural History Society of Brno on 8 February and 8 March 1865.

6.　Ibid.

7.　Robin Marantz Henig, *The Monk in the Garden: The Lost and Found Genius of Gregor Mendel, the Father of Genetics*, Houghton Mifflin Harcourt, May 2000, p. 17.

8.　Gregor Mendel, 'Experiments in Plant Hybridisation', translated by William Bateson, read at the Meetings of the Natural History Society of Brno on 8 February and 8 March 1865.

9.　Loren Cordain, 'Cereal Grains: Humanity's Double-Edged Sword', *World Review of Nutrition & Dietetics* 1999; 84, pp. 19–73.

10.　John J. Abel, 'Experimental and chemical studies of the blood with an appeal for more extended chemical training for the biological and medical investigator', *Science*, 6 August 1915, 42, p. 176.

11.　Joyce Carol Oates and Meghan O'Rourke, 'Why we write about grief', *New York Times*, 26 February 2011.

12.　M. Kaposi, *Pathology and Treatment of Diseases of the Skin for Practitioners and Students*, translation of the last German edition under the supervision of James C. Johnston, William Wood & Co., 1895, New York, pp. 479–80.

13.　Originally discovered in mice (P stands for pink-eyed dilution), this helps transport small molecules like tyrosine (which, as we have seen, is involved in melanin production).

14. 'Blue-Eyed Humans Have A Single, Common Ancestor', *ScienceDaily* (31 January 2008), http://www.sciencedaily.com/releases/2008/01/080130170343.htm, accessed 17 March 2012.

15. Hans Eiberg et al, 'Blue eye color in humans may be caused by a perfectly associated founder mutation in a regulatory element located within the HERC2 gene inhibiting OCA2 expression', *Human Genetics*, Vol. 123, No. 2, pp. 177–87.

16. 'Happy Hug a Ginga Day Off NZ', The Edge © 2012 MediaWorks Radio, http://www.theedge.co.nz/Events/HugaGingaDayOff2012.aspx, accessed 17 March 2012.

17. Maya Angelou, 'Human Family', *Scholastic Scope*, 52, 13 (23 February 2004), p. 21

18. Mark Dummett, 'India Facebook users urged to "appear whiter"', BBC News, 14 July 2010, http://www.bbc.co.uk/news/world-south+asia-10634777, accessed 17 March 2012.

19. Adlai Stevenson Speech, 'The Atomic Future' (18 September 1952), quoted in Richard Harrity (ed.), *Speeches*, Random House, New York, 1952, p. 129.

20. Answers:

    1. The person most likely has two copies of mutated or non-working MC1R genes, which cause red hair and freckles. However, the green eyes are caused by either the SLC24A4 gene or the TYR gene.

    2. A version of the TYR gene, which is implicated in freckles in darker skin.

    3. Red hair is because of non-working version of MC1R gene, and the blue eyes because of non-working version of the OCA2 gene.

    4. Albinos of East Asian descent are usually because of changes in the SLC45A2 gene.

EIGHT

Warm Skin, Cold Heart?

'But there are always both cold-blooded and hot-blooded people in the world at once. Why shouldn't they get on well together? They do, really.'

'They are always in conflict. Cold blood always wants to subjugate all hot blood. And hot-blooded ones have great fits of exterminating the cold-blooded ones. But the cold-blooded ones are cunning, and they never rest till they have made servants of the hot-blooded ones. Then they go too far. Then comes the retribution: and it all starts again.'

'And the hot-blooded ones are always servants?'

'Ye Gods, No. Alexander was hot-blooded, so was Jesus, so was Socrates, so was Caesar, so was Tamerlane and Attila, and Peter the Great and Fredrick the Great and even Voltaire ...'

– D.H. Lawrence[1]

The sensory aspects of skin—its appreciation of touch and pain and the skin's role in thermoregulation—are under-appreciated. We tend to be blind to brutal facts. If we define temperature or heat as a measure of 'molecular motion', there is usually a limit beyond which an organism or animal cannot function. If these thermal changes persist, specific genes are expressed, i.e., activated in order to try and produce different isozymes, or protein enzymes, to attempt survival in the new environmental conditions. If you think about it, evolution has been affected by both high and low temperatures. Animals that live in extremely cold conditions, like some polar fish, even contain anti-freeze compounds! On the other hand, there are 'heat shock proteins' (HSP) that chaperone some molecules into inducing a degree of heat tolerance. There's nothing half-hearted about this meticulous business-like approach, even if the story of evolution appears to human eyes like a creator's disjointed scribbles in diaries, almost an invitation to someone who may eventually dot all the Is and cross all the Ts.

Essentially, to maintain an animal's body temperature, heat production must equal heat loss. In the past, people called animals warm- or cold-blooded. Then came the terms 'homeothermic' (of a constant body temperature; like humans), 'ectothermic' (dependent on external heat, usually from the sun; think beetles or turtles) or 'endothermic' (body heat is generated internally by metabolism; like in birds and mammals). Heat production can be increased in several ways: increasing muscular activity (physical exertion in humans, or a bird or insect flapping its wings), shivering and non-shivering heat production (where animals like marsupials or bears use fat stores). Fish and reptiles begin actively moving about to generate body heat when the temperature is low. Similarly, it's possible to reduce body heat by certain methods. Birds, for instance, can reduce body temperature by fluffing or lubricating their feathers. Mammals reduce heat by evaporation, either by sweating or panting. Reptiles may do the same by changing body colour with the help of reflective platelets located within their cells.

Human skin maintains body temperature in many ways, and sweating is an extremely effective way of losing heat. Human skin has around 1.5 million sweat glands, divided into 'eccrine' and 'apocrine' glands. Eccrine glands are found all over our bodies, and open directly onto the skin surface. These glands produce sweat that is watery, with very little fat and virtually no salt. Apocrine glands are located in hair-bearing areas like scalp, armpits and groins and open into hair follicles before they reach the skin surface. They are hence prone to bacterial colonization that can lead to body odour. In animals like dogs, most sweat glands are apocrine, hence the 'dog smell'. These glands in dogs have hormonal functions and secrete 'pheromones' to attract mates. Dogs have no eccrine, or conventional, sweat glands, except on the nose, which is why they cool down by panting, not sweating. This is why it is dangerous to cover the mouth of a dog, or muzzle a dog in hot environments like cars parked outdoors at midday—the dog's body, especially the brain, can reach dangerously high, even fatal, body temperatures under these circumstances.

We've discussed how genes appear in linked chains right through evolution, seemingly preparing bodily organs for future tasks. This also holds true for body heat conductivity (BHC) and the human genome. Firstly, in an individual cell, heat can be transferred between nucleus and cytoplasm. Secondly, circulating fluids, like blood and lymph, can move between areas of different temperatures in the body to modulate overall body heat. We saw earlier how DNA was packed around spools called histones, and densely packed like folded 'strings of beads' into structures called chromatin. In cells subjected to heat shock, the heat-shock proteins are preferentially allocated to clusters of granules around this chromatin, which creates a highly packaged 'core' called 'condensed chromatin'. This has a major effect on body heat conductivity. Many proteins have been identified in the pervasive fruit fly, drosophila, that seem to be connected to body heat stress. What this stress does is decrease the transcription (remember, this is the process of creating an RNA copy of the DNA) of most genes, and preferentially activate a group of genes referred to as heat shock genes.

In the evolution of skin as a thermal regulatory organ, researchers feel that the assemblage of the greatest amount of condensed chromatin in *Homo sapiens* (when compared to other primates) was a turning point in the body's 'preparation' for thermoregulation, as this directly led to skin becoming less hairy or 'naked'. Taking this beyond thermoregulation, the loss of hair from the palms increased the creatures' ability to handle tools and therefore increased creative skills. This served a twofold purpose: as these primitive humans lived in Africa, where the sun was harsh, an increase in using tools and instruments increased both body heat conductivity and heat production (the latter due to increased physical activity, which in turn led to a larger brain). The fact that *skin and brain cells are formed at the same time*—in the ninth to twelfth week of embryo formation—is confirmation of this evolutionary link between a naked ape and a larger brain, as also of skin's role as a sense organ.

As primitive humans lost hair, the heat-preserving function of hair passed from hairy skin to the fat layer under the skin. As skin became a major regulator of body temperature, by developing more eccrine sweat glands to dissipate heat, it realized that it was no longer just a barrier but a full-fledged sense organ; one that needed an analysing brain to make sense of this new-found capability.

The evolution of temperature regulation is interesting. Even primitive creatures, say protozoa like paramecium, show abilities to sense temperature, and move to preferred temperatures. Researchers have found that the paramecium regulates temperature by using calcium or potassium channels located within its receptors. As multicellular organisms developed nerves and nervous systems, they developed neurons, aptly named thermoreceptors, that are sensitive to changes in temperature. When organisms moved from being unicellular to multicellular, the focus shifted from individual thermoregulation to temperature regulation of the entire colony.

> First of all he said to himself: 'That buzzing-noise means something. You don't get a buzzing-noise like that, just buzzing and buzzing, without meaning something. If there's a buzzing-noise, somebody's making a buzzing-noise, and the only reason for making a buzzing-noise that I know of is because you're a bee.'
>
> – A.A. Milne (*Winnie the Pooh*)[2]

Honey bees are interesting to study in this context because they are well organized, socially and physiologically, and their focus is on thermoregulation of the hive (especially brooding hives) and not each individual.

In summer, worker bees collect and fill water in the empty cells within the brood chamber, and then fan these 'tanks' vigorously with their wings to cool the water. These 'water bees' are specialized workers for whom this is the only assigned task; they don't actually participate in pollen- or nectar-foraging. While they cool the hive, a line of bees stretches across the entrance, fanning their wings vigorously, taking care to face the same way so that the cool air wafts across the young waiting to be nurtured. In winter, when the temperature drops, 'heater bees' take centre stage. These bees contract the muscles in their thorax—muscles that are usually used for flying, except that these bees are 'at rest'—generating heat using a combination of shivering and muscle contraction. Donor bees keep bringing food to these heater bees, essentially refuelling them, so they maintain their efficiency as 'heaters'.

It was this recognition that the body generated heat that led to the concept of 'hot' and 'cold' foods in Eastern cultures, especially in forms of medicine like Ayurveda. Certain foods like garlic, chicken and cloves are considered 'hot'. However, when scientifically measured, this heat had little to do with actual temperatures of the food or the person eating it. Yoghurt and oranges were considered 'cold'. The nature of a food, according to Ayurvedic medicine, can be modified; for example, adding garlic makes a food 'hotter'.

Lavoisier, the first man to coin the word 'oxygen', also spoke of *calorique* (caloric) values and *chaleur* (heat) in 1789. He was a pioneer in the context of relating physical work (or movement against gravity) to energy expenditure. However, before he could fully develop his ideas, he was guillotined by French revolutionaries. Eventually, as the metric system gained prominence, the term 'calorie' came to be officially adopted:[3]

> When substances endowed with considerable chemical affinity for each other combine chemically, much heat is developed [...] We shall estimate the quantity of heat thus set free by the number of kilogrammes of water which it would heat 1°C. The quantity of heat necessary to raise 1 kilogramme of water 1 degree is called a unit of heat, Calorie.[4]

Atwater, a chemist, and Rosa, a physicist, developed the first human calorimeter. They created a sealed chamber where the study subject ate, slept and worked on a bicycle. Sixteen staff worked round the clock to keep this chamber airtight. Water circulated in pipes so that heat produced by the body was absorbed by the water, and the temperature was measured using a combination of a thermometer and microscope (the latter to measure rise in water level as per earlier definition). Atwater studied the energy produced by different food sources and the energy expended by different activities. His experiments form the basis of modern dietary and calorie-counting advice. Suits worn by modern astronauts are nothing more than 'suit calorimeters' that maintain gas exchange and energy balance.

The Atwater calorimeter (*see plate*) does indeed look like a claustrophobic copper-lined torture chamber—no wonder it came equipped with a panic button! In actual fact, Atwater was looking at this body heat concept from an economic or industrial perspective. Would some foods generate more heat and therefore energy? Does each task expend different amounts of energy: for example, would mental tasks also use up energy? Could people be paid by valuing energy expenditure or heat production? Atwater used this business case to further his research. Given that he first got the idea of measuring the body's heat and energy expenditure during his study in Germany, it is fitting that Atwater's machine was more than capable of Germanic precision—it was said that if his volunteers as much as stopped to change the time on a watch, the calorimeter would register a change or lowering in heat output.

Whatever Atwater's calorimeter was developed to measure, his device helped understand the metabolism of creatures, the heat these metabolic processes generated and how skin regulated body heat. Further improvements have led to greater understanding of the mechanism of fever and regulation of body temperature.

The calorimeter played a very important role in the study of thermoregulation in animals. Here, finally, was technology that allowed us to measure the changes in body heat during different activities.

> In the depth of winter, I finally learned that within me there lay an invincible summer.
>
> –Albert Camus[5]

Skin plays a complex and multifaceted role in maintaining body temperature. The human body tends to maintain a temperature between 36°C and 38°C, and 37°C is considered 'normal'. Interestingly, the body's skin temperature is higher during sleep, which is why bedclothes usually have a higher insulation value. This increased skin temperature is because our basal metabolic rate (BMR, which is essentially the energy expended by an animal at rest) is lower during sleep.

To standardize metabolism studies, a unit has been created to measure metabolic rates: met (short for 'metabolic equivalent). 1 met $= 58.15$ W/m^2 (watts per square metre). A person has a BMR of 0.7 met when sleeping; 2 met when walking slowly, 4 to 8 met when swimming, and 8 to 12 met when playing tennis.

Why did organisms need to regulate temperature in the first place?

As we discussed, an ectotherm—an amphibian for instance—has virtually no ability to regulate its body temperature by itself, and so has to rely on the environment. For this, it largely has to adapt behavioural changes. It may therefore move into the sun to get warmer or burrow under soil to get cooler. Not very different from the way we seek shelter under a shade in the hot midday sun—except we are not totally dependent on the environment for our body heat. These behavioural mechanisms make for interesting study. Frogs, for instance, can move to warmer areas when temperatures are low. This active movement in itself causes muscle movement, which increases body temperature. Amphibians like frogs have thin skin and therefore low body temperatures, usually below 20^0C. Turtles, on the other hand, have thick skin. While thick skin does not lose heat by sweat evaporation easily, turtles have developed the ability to change circulation or *increase skin blood flow*, thereby controlling temperature. Reptiles generally live in drier and warmer climes, and their body temperature is higher. Even though fish generate heat, most of this energy is lost through the water leaving their gills. Because of this, fish rely on a sodium (Na^+) pump to supply energy and thus counteract the heat loss. (We will discuss the sodium pump a little later.) Thyroxine, the thyroid hormone that humans also use to control metabolic rates, seems to control this sodium pump in animals. Thyroxine is involved in hair moulting, hair and wool growth and also controls the metabolic rate and thereby heat production.

One of the fundamental reasons why the body must regulate heat is to optimize the action of enzymes during metabolic processes: which is to say, enzymes function best within certain narrow temperature ranges. For best physiological performance, an animal's body temperature must be kept within these limits. Towards ensuring this, skin and the hypothalamus of the brain play important roles (*see Figure 25*).

The energy for life function is generated by ATP (adenosine tri-phosphate), which is rather like the currency of living forces. ATP is present in both the cytoplasm and the nucleus, and every metabolic process uses this stored ATP for energy production.

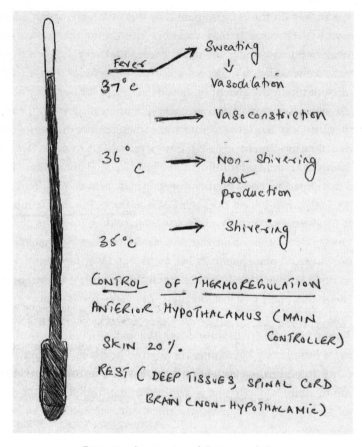

FIGURE 25   An overview of thermoregulation

Therefore, the body generates a continuous supply of ATP; it is estimated that the human body produces more than 150kg of ATP daily. Even single-celled primitive creatures produce ATP. Viruses, though, cannot produce ATP, and therefore rely on the host RNA to supply them with energy. Specific 'uncoupling proteins' have been discovered in the family of mitochondrial transporters. These uncoupling proteins create a proton leak at the mitochondrial membrane, which results in increased respiratory activity and more heat generation.

Essentially, fever is caused due to a 'resetting' of the body thermostat due to infection or disease, and in most animals a fever greater than 6°C above normal can prove fatal. But how is this thermostat regulated?

Human beings can sense different levels of cold and heat due to special spots or receptors—thermoreceptors—located in the skin and the hypothalamus of the brain. These thermoreceptors are located in the dermis at various depths: 0.15 mm to 0.17 mm deep for cold receptors (immediately below the epidermis) and 0.3 mm to 0.6 mm deep for warm receptors (upper layer of the dermis). The shallowness of the cold spots relative to warm spots means that humans are generally more sensitive to cold than they are to heat. Also, a person feels colder or hotter when the temperature of skin falls or rises than when it is constant, because stimulation fades after the initial shock of temperature change. This is why you feel extremely cold on entering a cold swimming pool; the 'overreaction' settles down after a period when the body has had some time to adjust its metabolism.

Skin also controls temperature by altering blood supply (*see Figure 26*). When it is cold, for example, there is reduced blood circulation to the skin because the blood vessels constrict (vasoconstriction). In the epidermis and upper dermis, in fact, thermal resistance or heat conductance determines heat flow. Below the capillaries, our skin contains small vein networks (venous plexuses) that are in turn fed by arterioles (small arterial networks). In the feet and hands, additional arteriovenous (AV) anastomoses—connections, or links between arteries and veins—also alter blood flow, and thereby temperature. For example, when we exercise and our bodies are hot, nerves on the receptors stimulate these AV anastomoses to open, and they rapidly supply warm arterial blood to the veins, which promotes heat loss by conduction.

Joon-Ho Choi, assistant professor of engineering at Missouri University of Science and Technology, spent his student days working in an intensive care unit to study the skin's role in thermoregulation.

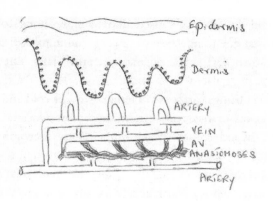

FIGURE 26   Thermoregulation through blood flow

He wondered if body sensors on patients could help set the room temperature, rather than the preference of nurses or doctors. He found the inner arm best suited to the placement of a specially developed sensor that could help regulate a room's thermostat, so that the room would be at optimum temperature for patients. Choi realized that the body has many biosignals, and each signal is virtually a message to the environment.

Warm-blooded creatures keep core temperatures relatively constant by using a 'counter-current' heat transfer system between arteries and veins, whereby warm arterial blood can transfer heat to the cool venous blood. This counter-current system has many forms: in our arms and legs, we have one artery and one vein alongside each other, and in our fingers, we have one artery surrounded by many veins. (This latter system is similar to the one found in whales' fins, reflecting the fact that primitive whales once lived on land.) Some animals, like dogs, have *rete mirabilis*—a system of hundreds of arteries and veins running parallely and intermingling—especially around the nasal passages, which helps them cool down by panting.

If the skin's efficient counter-current system is used to regulate body heat, can an industrial counter-current system utilize heat from the human body? This was the question that a Swedish real estate company pondered a few years ago. Jernhusen AB, the

Swedish company, planned to harness the body heat generated by humans in Stockholm's railway station to warm their nearby office building. They have developed a system that uses hot air from human bodies to warm water, which is pumped through pipes to the building next door. Karl Sundholm, who was instrumental in developing the project, felt that 250,000 people passing through the station could power around a tenth of the building's heating needs. Rufus Ford of Sustainable Energy Action in London thinks this might be worth considering for London's Tube as it is 'always warm down there'.

Our hands have the most sensitive response to our body's thermoregulation. In warm conditions, the blood vessels of the hands are dilated, and hence our fingertips are the warmest parts. When the hands are cold, the blood vessels are constricted, and the temperature differential between hands and the trunk can be as much as 8°C. When 'finger temperatures' are below 15°C, the fingers become less dexterous.

The neck, in contrast, has the highest skin temperature of any body part when a person is cold. This is how the habit of wearing a scarf or turning up a jacket collar came to be—to reduce the loss of heat due to a bigger temperature differential.

Skin temperature rises during and just before sleep, and conversely, body core temperature decreases as the body's metabolism slows. To prevent heat loss, people cover themselves to create a climate of 34°C, which they would generally find too hot when awake. Therefore, increasing skin temperature makes people sleepy, which is why we give babies a warm bath before bedtime, and why warming the feet is especially effective if one does not sleep well or is having difficulty sleeping.

Older people have a lower body temperature. Longevity genes identified in mice, including Prop-1 and Pit-1, are implicated in both lowered body temperature and increased lifespan. Studies on older people suggest calorie restriction, and therefore less obesity, which also causes lowering of body temperature.

When we shiver, the body is trying to conserve its heat by constricting skin blood vessels. If this fails, the body contracts muscles to increase heat, which is why our teeth begin to chatter.

Fat people shiver less as they have more insulation provided by fat tissue. Another reason is because the body works harder to carry the extra 'load'; therefore, the fatter the person, the more heat he or she generates through metabolic processes. This rise in core temperature makes an overweight person sweat more than a lean counterpart. Sweating through the body's eccrine sweat glands is regulated primarily by the hypothalamus of the brain. Of course, the threshold for sweat production is also modified by the skin temperature. At a given core body temperature, warmer skin temperature induces more sweating, while colder skin temperature inhibits it. However, body core temperature is five to ten times more influential than skin temperature when it comes to controlling sweating. Interestingly, and contrary to popular wisdom, women actually have less body fluid than men and are therefore more prone to dehydration. This means that their bodies conserve more water and therefore women sweat less than men. Researchers feel testosterone levels (lower in women) may have something to do with this.

The importance of the skin's sweating mechanism—and indeed of skin's role in thermoregulation in an active animal—was accentuated when Yannas and Burke developed the first artificial skin. While artificial skin performed virtually all other functions of skin, it could not sweat, therefore limiting the physical activity that its recipients could do.

When physical work increases and body heat rises, the skin's sweating mechanism responds by recruiting more sweat glands to participate, and then making each gland increase its production (*see Figure 27*).

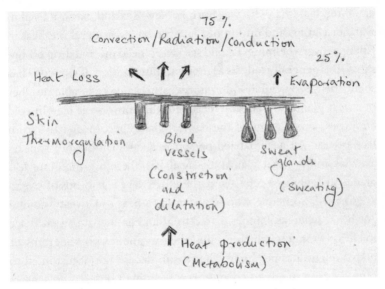

FIGURE 27   The skin's thermoregulation mechanism

His hair is crisp, and black, and long,
His face is like the tan:
His brow is wet with honest sweat,
He earns whate'er he can,
And looks the whole world in the face,
For he owes not any man.

> – from 'The Village Blacksmith' by
> Henry Wadsworth Longfellow

At the onset of sweat production, as Longfellow noted, the first area to sweat is the forehead, followed by upper arms, hands, thighs, feet and then the trunk. On our cheeks and over the cheekbones, the skin has a higher temperature to help evaporation of sweat running down the forehead.

Sweat glands also play an interesting role in a person's acclimatization to heat. I was born in England and grew up in India, mostly in the country's warm south. I have lived equally in the West and East, and generally cope well with both heat and cold. My daughter, Natasha, who was born in New Zealand, has not lived in warmer climes, and during our last trip to India found the heat in Chennai overwhelming. I could see sweat 'bead up' and drop off her skin—this generally reflects a lack of acclimatization. If someone has spent their early childhood in hot weather, a considerable number of sweat glands are already recruited; the converse is true in cold countries, where many of these sweat glands become inactive from lack of use. An acclimatized person may sweat more but appears drier as more sweat glands are available, therefore there are less glands struggling to cope—and, therefore, very few 'beads of sweat' are formed. Someone who is not used to heat can sweat one litre per hour, whereas someone used to a hot climate can sweat twice to thrice as much, which is equivalent to about two kilograms of body weight loss per hour. The reason people not accustomed to humid heat struggle to cope is because human skin has no sensors that detect humidity, and if skin 'wetness' increases beyond 25 per cent due to extremely humid weather, the epidermis swells as it absorbs moisture. This swelling triggers mechanoreceptors (nerves which respond to mechanical changes like stretching of tissue due to swelling) in the nerves, making the person feel unpleasant or uncomfortable.

The other interesting fact is that if an area of skin remains completely wet for a few hours, the sweat rate will drop off—an effect called hidromeiosis—in order to reduce unproductive water loss, because fully wet skin cannot further evaporate.

Our palms and soles have a large number of eccrine sweat glands, but they are not useful for heat regulation. In fact, they are rather more excited by emotional stimuli—a fact utilized by 'lie-detector tests', which measure the electrical resistance of the skin when these glands are activated.

Somehow, it was hotter then. Men's stiff collars wilted by nine in the morning. Ladies bathed before noon and after their three o'clock naps. And by nightfall were like soft teacakes with frosting from sweating and sweet talcum. The day was twenty-four hours long, but it seemed longer.[6]

If you were to ask the skin to summarize thermoregulation, it would simply say two words: 'inner fire'. It would then explain that its warmth is connected to interior molecular states, defence mechanisms, emotional feelings and changes of environment. After all, a candle cannot burn without a fire. Such is the flicker of life.

NOTES

1. D.H. Lawrence and Freida Lawrence, *The First Lady Chatterley*, The Dial Press Inc., 1944, USA, p. 178.

2. A.A. Milne, *Winnie the Pooh: The Complete Collection of Stories and Poems*, Methuen Children's Books, 1994.

3. James L. Hargrove, 'History of the Calorie in Nutrition', *The Journal of Nutrition*, Vol. 136, No. 12, pp. 2957–2961.

4. Calorie is capitalized when the text refers to a kg-calorie and in lower case when it refers to a g-calorie; Calorie = 4.1868 kJ.

5. Albert Camus, as quoted in Nathan A. Scott, *The Unquiet Vision: Mirrors of Man in Existentialism*, The World Publishing Company, 1969, p. 116.

6. Harper Lee, *To Kill a Mockingbird*, Arrow Books Ltd, 50th Anniversary Edition, 2010.

NINE

Touching God

Who taught you to write in blood on my back? Who taught you to use your hands as branding irons? You have scored your name into my shoulders, referenced me with your mark. The pads of your fingers have become printing blocks, you tap a message on to my skin, tap meaning into my body.

— Jeanette Winterson[1]

Ludwig Feuerbach, the German philosopher and anthropologist, once said that the sense of touch was atheist from birth. From a philosophical point of view, I guess he meant: if God exists, I must be able to touch him. Denis Diderot, who proclaimed something similar on his deathbed, famously debated the 'Molyneux Problem'. The question it poses is this—whether a man born blind, who comes to enjoy the sense of vision later, on seeing a cube and a sphere, without being able to touch them, would he be able to distinguish the objects? The answer is essentially a discussion on vision being two-dimensional and subject to optical illusions, unlike touch.

John Bramblitt stumbled across the answer in his early twenties. He was sideswiped by a car and lost his vision. Still, two decades of seeing objects had provided him a visual memory of images he wanted to paint. Rendering these images on a canvas proved a challenge, until he discovered 'puffy paint'—the kind of paint that is used to decorate fabric and leaves a line that Bramblitt could feel. He felt the outlines with his left hand, and began to fill in colours using a brush held in his right hand. Now, if you ask Bramblitt, he says that white *feels* thicker on the fingers, like toothpaste, while black feels slicker. Research has shown that irrespective of whether he or she was trained in Braille, in a blind person, the brain's visual cortex is reassigned to other senses, like touch. This cross-modal plasticity results in blind people having a much better sense of touch, because the brain uses touch to 'see'—quite literally, by commandeering the visual areas to the sense of touch. John Bramblitt's paintings are vibrant, almost psychedelic. The brilliance of his paintings is such that you forget he is blind. One of my favourites is 'Mikey' (*see plate section*).

However, as humans, we fear losing sight more than any other sensation. This is why the Greek Aristoteles, or Aristotle (384–322 BC), considered sight as the basis for contemplation. In *Metaphysics* he wrote:[2]

> All men naturally desire knowledge. An indication of this is our esteem for the senses; for apart from their use we esteem them for their own sake, and most of all the sense of sight. Not only with a view to action, but even when no action is contemplated, we prefer sight, generally speaking, to all the other senses. The reason for this is that of all the senses sight best helps us to know things, and reveals many distinctions.
>
> Now animals are by nature born with the power of sensation, and from this some acquire the faculty of memory, whereas others do not.

Interestingly, touch—not sight—is the first sensory system to develop. The sense of touch is one of the primary functions of skin. The first sensory inputs from skin come in when the baby is still in the womb, and touch continues to be the primary means of learning or experiencing the world in infancy and childhood. The skin has many sensory receptors that modulate this sense of touch, and we will discuss those anatomical aspects later in this chapter. The sense of touch continues to function even after sight and hearing have failed, as often happens with advanced age.

In recognition of this fact, Aristotle considered touch as the *only* essential sense, from an existential point of view. He felt that senses like taste and smell were necessary for well-being, but not for being—but when touch was destroyed, so was life. In *De Anima*, Aristotle wrote:[3]

It is clear that the body of an animal cannot be simple, i.e., consist of one element, such as fire or air. For without touch, it is impossible to have any other sense; for every body that has soul in it must, as we have said, be capable of touch. All the other elements with the exception of earth can constitute organs of sense, but all of them bring about perception only through something else, viz., through the media. Touch takes place by direct contact with its objects, whence also its name. All the other organs of sense, no doubt, perceive by contact, only the contact is mediate: touch alone perceives by immediate contact. Consequently no animal body can consist of these other elements.

Nor can it consist solely of earth. For touch is as it were a mean between all tangible qualities, and its organ is capable of receiving not only all the specific qualities which characterize earth, but also the hot and the cold and all other tangible qualities whatsoever. That is why we have no [...] sensation by means of bones, hair, &c., because they consist of earth. So too plants, because they consist of earth, have no sensation. Without touch there can be no other sense, and the organ of touch cannot consist of earth or of any other single element.

It is evident, therefore, that the loss of this one sense alone must bring about the death of an animal. For as on the one hand nothing which is not an animal can have this sense, so on the other it is the only one which is indispensably necessary to what is an animal.

[...]

All the other senses are necessary to animals, as we have said, not for their being, but for their well-being. Such, e.g., is sight, which, since it lives in air or water, or generally in what is pellucid, it must have in order to see, and taste because of what is pleasant or painful to it, in order that it may perceive these qualities in its nutriment and so may desire to be set in motion, and hearing that it may have communication made to it, and a tongue that it may communicate with its fellows.

Johann Gottfried Herder, in his work *Sculpture: Some Observations on Shape and Form from Pygmalion's Creative Dream*, also argued that the sense of touch is actually more important than sight to appreciate art or sculpture. Is this really true? This was a question Zeng Bailiang, vice chairman of the Nanning Artists Association and noted art teacher, had grappled with ever since he first picked up a paintbrush in 1971, at the age of twelve. He saw a young boy of four sitting beside him and asked him what he wanted him to paint.

'I would like you to paint that bird over there, in the bushes, the one with the long beak and green back,' the boy replied. Zeng squinted his eyes, but could not see any bird. He walked up to the bush and moved some branches aside, and to his surprise, he found a bird that had a green back and a long beak. His surprise turned to wonder when he realized that this was no four-year-old with great eyesight, this was a four-year-old with *no* eyesight. The kid was blind. He asked the young boy how he knew that there was a bird when he had no eyesight. 'It is there. I can *feel* it,' the boy replied.

This life-changing experience impelled Zeng Bailiang to develop painting classes for people with visual impairment. When sceptics doubted him, he arranged competitions in needle-threading between the blind and the able-sighted. The blind always won.

By now, Zeng has tutored more than 30,000 blind artists in China. He takes his students on walks so they can touch flowers and leaves and understand textures. To help them choose colours, he uses scents to guide them. For example, in Zeng's class, the yellow paints are lemon-scented, green pigments smell of grass, and red colours smell like roses. He merely teaches the students how to measure the water they add to the ink. 'We overly trust what we see, but the blind use other senses to set their minds free,' he says.

> I am struck by how integral tactile actions and symbols are to social life. Touch is not just a private act. It is a fundamental medium for the expression, experience and the contestation of social values and hierarchies. The culture of touch involves all of culture.
>
> – Constance Classen[4]

All of culture? Does this include bacterial cultures? No, really, I'm not jesting. If the sense of touch is indispensable for life—and we have been saying all creatures are linked genetically and have semi-permeable membrane coverings—do primitive or microscopic organisms such as bacteria 'feel' touch? As a young medical student studying human microbiology for the first time, I was astounded to learn that the 'normal' human body hosted many bacteria, even if they did not cause a clinical infection.

When I teach cutaneous surgery, I tell my students that it takes 10^5 or 100,000 bacterial organisms to cause a wound infection. In the presence of a skin suture, one needs only 10^2 or 100 organisms to cause a skin infection. This is why, when a surgical wound gets infected, it is usually at the site where the suture knots are located, and the response that leads to the infection is initially triggered by a 'foreign body reaction'. The most common skin pathogen is *Staphylococcus aureus*, just as the most common urinary bacterium is *Escherichia coli*. If you observed human urine under the microscope, you would see very many bacteria. But unless the organism count reaches 100,000, it does not result in a clinical infection. When Christopher Hayes, associate professor of molecular, cellular and development biology at the University of California (Santa Barbara) (UCSB), and his team studied *Escherichia coli*, they discovered a sibling-like link between cell systems that had largely been thought of as rivals; the bacteria seemed to communicate by contact or touch.

Bacteria have a contact-dependent inhibition system (CDI), which is designed to inhibit or kill other bacteria. Hayes's team at UCSB found that bacteria with CDI can inhibit bacteria without such a system only if the target bacteria have CysK, a metabolic enzyme required for synthesis of cysteine, an amino acid. The study points to the enzyme CysK as the potential catalyst to such bacterial communication—like a secret handshake, or code. Hayes has been quoted as saying, 'If you have the right credentials, you're allowed into the club; otherwise you're turned away. There's a velvet rope, if you will, and if you're not one of the cool kids, you can't get in.'

David Low, professor at UCSB, praises this work on contact-dependent enzymes as ground-breaking. He was recently quoted as saying, 'We are just starting to get some clues that bacteria may be talking to each other with a contact-dependent language. They touch and respond to one another in different ways depending on the CDI systems and other genotypic factors. Our hope is that ultimately this work may aid the development of drugs that block or enhance touch-dependent communication, whether the bacteria is harmful or helpful.'

While Hayes's team only studied the urinary pathogen *E. coli*, as they are easy to study, their finding suggests that bacteria may indeed communicate by touch or contact.

> Someone should write a book on the epistemology of the sense of touch
>
> – J. Bennett[5]

Aristotle claimed plants, unlike animals, were passive creatures and therefore insensitive to touch. In the 'natural ladder' of life or *scala naturae*, he felt that 'plants are created for the sake of animals' and 'animals for the sake of men'. This was the pervading philosophy until the nineteenth century, when Erasmus Darwin, grandfather of Charles Darwin, suggested to his grandson that he should study plants.

Like human skin, plant epidermis possesses a clear single-cell-thick 'cuticle' layer, similar to the *stratum lucidum* on the palms and soles of humans. In 1917, Professor Winthrop John VanLeuven Osterhout, professor of botany at Harvard University, decided to compare the barrier function and nutrient exchange properties of laminaria (golden seaweed) and frog skins, and was stunned to find that both creatures' skins showed similar properties: an increase in permeability when soaked in some compounds, like calcium chloride, and a decrease in others, like salt water. Both showed cell death when submerged in salt water for prolonged periods, with similar 'death curves'. In other words, both plant and animal skins functioned as efficient barriers and also participated in exchange or absorption of nutrients.

Aristotle opined that what defined an animal's 'life' was its skin's sense of touch. But, as we just discussed, plants have a covering resembling skin, and plant skin has an epidermal layer. Does this mean plants can sense touch?

Rapid responses by plants to touch are actually well known and generally classified as thigmotropic or thigmonastic. (*Thigma* in Greek is touch; 'tropism' signifies that the response to touch is in the direction of the stimulus, such as a climbing plant; 'nastic' behaviour occurs independent of direction, such as the folding leaves of a 'touch-me-not'.) Recent advances in comparative biology also show that plant cells communicate via chemical messengers and have hormone-like neurochemicals, such as auxin.

Figure 28 shows a nerve cell or neuron. The axon, which is the long projection from the cell, transmits impulses rather like an electric cable. Axons connect with other nerve cells and sometimes to glands and muscles through junctions called synapses.

The theory that plants can feel sensations seems incorrect: how

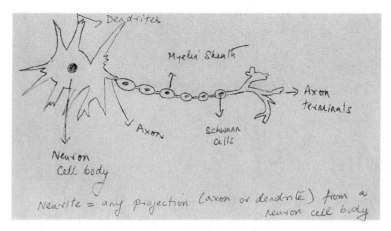

FIGURE 28   Structure of a nerve cell

can walled cells support transmission of impulses over distances if there are no axons or synaptic junctions that permit a neuron to send electrical or chemical signals to other cells or neurons?

Many scientists now think that the acellular phloem, which carries nutrients to all parts of a plant, and spans its entire length, is most likely to play the role of axons in animal cells. After all, plants make many neuroactive substances. For example, in response to wounding, plants make the hormone ethylene, which also acts as an anaesthetic. Stunningly, a hormone found in plants, abscisic acid, is also found in sponges and in the brains of rats and pigs. I wonder what Darwin would have made of this recent discovery. A triumphal smile might have creased his face. Darwin, you see, was especially fascinated by carnivorous plants like the sundew, *Drosera rotundifolia*. Its tentacles are so sensitive that they can differentiate an insect leg from a human hair. Remarkably, this plant is able to distinguish stimuli unrelated to food, like rain and wind, and remains unmoved when confronted by such stimuli. An insect, on the other hand, is rarely spared.

In his last book, *The Power of Movement in Plants* (1880), Charles Darwin closed with a (then) controversial statement, when he compared the root apex of plants to the brains of lower animals:[6]

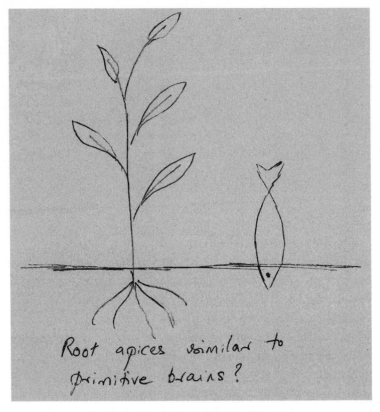

Root apices similar to primitive brains?

FIGURE 29   My schematic depiction of Darwin's
controversial statement

It is hardly an exaggeration to say that the tip of the radicle thus
endowed [with sensitivity] and having the power of directing the
movements of the adjoining parts, acts like the brain of one of the
lower animals; the brain being seated within the anterior end of the
body, receiving impressions from the sense-organs, and directing
the several movements.

Recently, several researchers have demonstrated that roots can
not only search for water and nutrition, but also actively avoid
dangerous soil patches, and also sometimes attack and kill other
competing roots by exuding toxins.

Adam is fading out. It is on account of Darwin and that crowd. I can see that he is not going to last much longer. There's a plenty of signs. He is getting belittled to a germ—a little bit of a speck that you can't see without a microscope powerful enough to raise a gnat to the size of a church. They take that speck and breed from it: first a flea, then a fly, then a bug, then cross these and get a fish, then a raft of fishes, all kinds, then cross the whole lot and get a reptile, then work up the reptiles till you've got a supply of lizards and spiders and toads and alligators and Congressmen and so on, then cross the entire lot again and get a plant of amphibiums, which are half-breeds and do business both wet and dry, such as turtles and frogs and ornithorhyncuses and so on, and cross-up again and get a mongrel bird, sired by a snake and dam'd by a bat, resulting in a pterodactyl, then they develop him, and water his stock till they've got the air filled with a million things that wear feathers, then they cross-up all the accumulated animal life to date and fetch out a mammal, and start-in diluting again till there's cows and tigers and rats and elephants and monkeys and everything you want down to the Missing Link, and out of him and a mermaid they propagate Man, and there you are! Everything ship-shape and finished-up, and nothing to do but lay low and wait and see if it was worth the time and expense.

– Mark Twain[7]

Erlangen, 1864. So is this how career choices are made—with a terrible loss of freedom? The son of a pharmacist, Friedrich Sigmund Merkel, a free spirit and lateral thinker, decided to join the navy and become a sailor. Towards his latter years at school, the young man had become dissatisfied with the pedantic nature of education, especially the nuances of grammar. 'It did not matter to me whether the indicative or the conjunctive had to be applied,' he said later.

The problem for Merkel was that too many young men were seeking the freedom the navy offered. His application was declined. He was forced to seek refuge in the comfort of known terrain:

medicine. His father, after all, was a pharmacist and his brother Johann, a surgeon. How far would the young Friedrich continue his studies? Even he did not know for certain. However, in 1865, he wrote to his mother that he really liked the study of medicine and all the subjects, barring one: anatomy. I am sure, he wrote, that I will never become an anatomist. Merkel did so well in his studies that his father sent him on a holiday to Belgium and Holland as a reward. When he returned, Merkel decided to continue his training at Greifswald. This was when he found his true love. He had assumed that love, when it consumed him, would be centred on a feminine object. After all, that was what usually happened. It was strange, this love at first sight. Exhilaration had overcome him as soon as he had peered into a fascinating new world—he had discovered the wonder of the microscope and a love of microscopic anatomy and pathology.

'*Das mikroskop ist eine grosse erfindung*' (The microscope is a great invention),[8] Merkel exclaimed. He pondered if it was an invention comparable to the steam engine, the printing press and the powder gun. All great inventions, he felt, had predecessors, but were differentiated from them by a sudden stroke of intellect, a rap of genius. After all, before printing presses were made with moveable type, there existed primitive presses. Similarly, the microscope evolved from the telescope; with the addition of achromatic lenses, it opened up a fascinating new micro-world. The physics of technology and the secrets of science this new device revealed convinced Merkel that it was truly one of the great inventions. He decided to write a book popularizing the microscope and to stimulate interest among both the educated and the curious.

In the late nineteenth century, Germany was infatuated with the microscope, which resulted in many scientists collaborating to develop methods of staining tissues for histological analysis (microscopic analyses of tissues). Böhmer and Fischer independently introduced the stains hematoxylin and eosin (H&E) in 1865 and 1875 respectively. As the idea of using double-staining techniques to provide contrast between the nucleus and cytoplasm took hold, Wissowzky described the combination of the haematoxylin and eosin dyes in 1876.

Haematoxylin is extracted from the Central American logwood tree *Haematoxylum campechianum*. The word 'haematoxylin' derives from Greek, meaning 'blood-like wood'. On its own, it cannot stain tissues. It is, therefore, oxidized by using certain oxidizing agents to 'ripen' the stain, after which a mordant (a substance used to 'set' dyes and intensify colours) is added. This dye stains tissues purple, which are made 'bluer' for better viewing by dipping in alkaline agents. Eosin is a fluorescent red dye (Eos is Greek goddess of 'dawn').

Nearly a century and a half later, H&E stains are still commonly used for histological analysis of tissues under the microscope; in fact, they are the 'bread-and-butter' stains for pathological analyses even today. Haematoxylin selectively stains nuclei and chromatin, and spares the cytoplasm; Eosin predominantly stains cytoplasmic structures. (See the *plate section* for the sort of images an H&E stain provides under a microscope.)

In keeping with this upsurge in 'microscopic vision', Friedrich Merkel published *Das Mikroskop and Seine Anwendung* (The Microscope and Its Applications) in 1875. That year he also went on to describe '*tastzellen*', or touch-sensitive cells in skin. These cells are what most medical students or doctors remember Merkel for—they are known as 'Merkel cells'.

Merkel felt that it was only logical that skin contained special receptors that responded to mechanical stimuli, such as touch or pressure. He asked: '*Warum, so fragt man billig, soil nun der fiinfte Sinn, der Tastsinn, nicht auch mit den gleichen Endapparaten versehen sein?*' (Why, as one might reasonably ask, should the fifth sense, that of touch, not be equipped with comparable terminal structures?)[9] He first studied the epidermis of ducks and geese. Merkel decided to 'fix' their epidermal tissue by using a different staining technique— osmic acid—for two to three weeks. Osmic acid is a crystalline oxide of osmium, the aqueous solution of which Merkel chose as a fixative because it selectively stains fat and myelin, which means it doesn't stain neurites (which are projections from the cell body). This allowed Merkel to identify little Tastkorperchen or 'touch bodies' independent from the neurites.

We know of two types of mechanoreceptors in skin (*see Figure 30*). One: rapidly acting mechanoreceptors, which respond by initiating a brief burst of impulses; for instance, when hair is moved or displacement of skin occurs around hair follicles. Two: slowly acting mechanoreceptors; like 'hair discs' (first described by Felix Pinkus as 'haarscheibe', or hair, in 1902), which are only excited by displacement of the disc itself, and not by movement of surrounding skin. Pinkus noted that these discs were similar to Romer's tubercles of the echidna (a spiny ant-eater found in Australia). Many hairy mammals have haarscheiben, but in rodents they seem to indicate directional movements of hair. Only in cats and humans do they serve as skin mechanoreceptors. Felix Pinkus's son, Hermann Pinkus, who also became a renowned dermatopathologist, claimed in 1974 that he could locate these 'hair discs' by probing skin with a blunt pencil. Usually, when the subject perceived a cool sensation rather than touch, a hair disc was found. Merkel cells are also slow-adapting, and fire at high frequency during mechanical displacement like sustained touch or pressure.

Merkel cells are widely prevalent in mammalian skin. In humans, these cells are found in glabrous skin, like the palms, where they cluster beneath the ridges that form fingerprints. There are usually around 50 cells per mm^2. In hairy skin, the Merkel cells are clustered in the outer root sheath of the hair follicle, where the arrector pili muscles (which help hair 'stand' and thereby help insulate human skin) attach, forming the so-called hair discs of Pinkus.

The evolutionary origin of the Merkel cell has fostered some debate amongst pathologists and dermatologists: *is this cell from skin or nerve?* The question has been fought over for more than two decades—the sort of scientific battle only a skin researcher could get up at night for. I guess there was some justification for

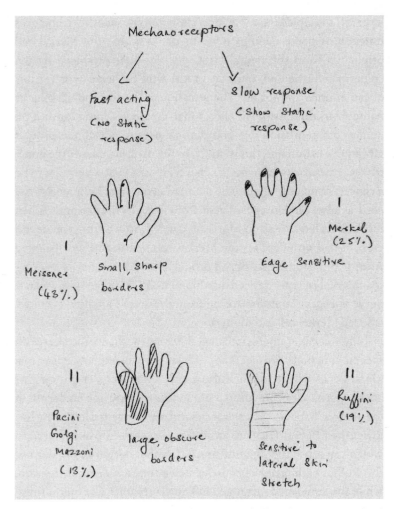

FIGURE 30   The function of different kinds
of mechanoreceptors

it, though, because a 'trabecular carcinoma' that was described in 1972 appeared to be a tumour of Merkel cells. A tumour can only be called a 'carcinoma' if it is of epithelial origin; therefore, this was really a debate on nomenclature.

It is a complex debate. We know these cells are found in the basal layer of the epidermis, but don't Merkel cell–neurite complexes function as nerve endings? One theory was that the Merkel cell originated from the neural crest and was later produced by the epidermis. In the end, once again, the fruit fly helped answer this question once and for all. The atonal gene[10] in drosophila gets its name from the disruptive effects that the gene's mutation has on neuron differentiation into chordotonal organs, which sense sound vibrations. In humans, this is similar to the Atoh-1—part of the notch pathway we discussed in earlier chapters—and is now thought to be a cancer 'switch-off' gene. The neurons in our hind brain and spinal cord as also Merkel cells derive from this Atoh-1 lineage. When researchers led by Kristin Morrison deleted Atoh-1 from the neural crest, it had no effect on the Merkel cell population, but deleting Atoh-1 from skin cells stopped production of Merkel cells, proving that Merkel cells are derived developmentally from the skin, and not nerve lineages. Tumours arising from these cells are now correctly labelled Merkel cell carcinomas.

In human skin, there are a few different mechanoreceptors with specific functions (*see Figure 31*). We have discussed how epidermal Merkel cells detect touch and pressure. Meissner's corpuscles, or 'tactile corpuscles', are located immediately below the epidermis in the dermal papillae. These mechanoreceptors sense light touch—lower than 50 Hz. They are located in glabrous skin, like fingertips, which can sense the slightest touch. Located deeper in the dermis, the Ruffini endings or corpuscles detect tension deep in the skin, while the lamellated (arranged in lamellae, rather like onion rings) Pacinian corpuscles detect rapid vibrations—around 200–300 Hz.

I'd mentioned earlier that touch is the first human sensation to develop. The late Ashley Montagu, who was a great anthropologist and student of the evolution of touch, reported responses to the stroking of an eight-week-old foetus's cheek with hairs—this kind of light touch sensation is usually the earliest to develop.

We have discussed thermoregulation in previous chapters, and now the mechanism of touch, but do they affect each other? In 1846,

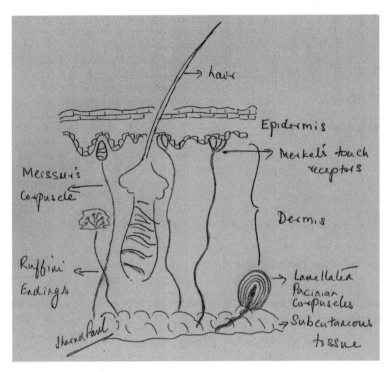

FIGURE 31   Mechanoreceptors in human skin

Weber suggested that a cold dollar (*'thaler'* in German, in Weber's original description) placed on his forehead felt approximately as heavy as two warm dollars. Weber surmised that cold strengthens and warmth lightens pressure sensations (which we know are detected by Merkel cells). Was he right? Whether he was or not, this theory went unchallenged until the 1970s, when experiments to test Weber's theories revealed the following: cold does intensify pressure sensation, and the colder the object, the heavier it feels. In extreme cold conditions, a 10g feels the same as a 100g weight in warm conditions. Warmth can intensify pressure, but minimally, and only on the forearm and not the forehead (therefore Weber was partly wrong). The converse does not apply, i.e., changing the force of pressure does not alter sense of cold or warmth. (The warmth and cold referred to here is the temperature of the objects and not ambient temperature; warm and cold ambient temperatures seem to make sensations more acute, but that might just be a reflection of the change in temperature of the mechanoreceptors themselves.)

THE GIFT OF PAIN

> God is a concept by which
> we measure our pain.
>
> – John Lennon[11]

We know now that the skin is a highly complex nerve-filled organ with a wide array of mechanical receptors. To become who we are, to form our habits and behaviours, we need to interact with our environment. The sense of touch is a big part of that curiosity. And pain is important in ensuring that our inquisitiveness does not end in calamity.

Think for a moment of an infant crawling on the floor exploring a room. If the infant picks up a hot object, it instinctively drops the object because of the unpleasant sensation. If a burn were to result, the impact would be far less than if the sensation of pain was absent.

A Case History[12]

PS, a male child, was first seen when eight months of age by the casualty officer at the Memorial Hospital, Woolwich, where his mother had taken him because he had bitten his fingers to such an extent that medical treatment was required. At a loss to explain the condition and how to deal with the persistent biting, the casualty officer referred the child to the paediatric department. Apart from these self-inflicted injuries, the child had at no time shown any discomfort, let alone pain, and his mother recalled he had not reacted to his inoculations as other children do. Clinically, he was a robust, healthy child, the firstborn of healthy young unrelated parents; the pregnancy and delivery had been uneventful and until the time he began to injure himself, they had had no concern about him. Routine examination revealed no abnormality apart from the demonstrable failure to react to normally pain-producing stimuli, such as pressure on the tendon Achilles, testicular pressure or jabbing the skin with a sharp instrument. A presumptive diagnosis of congenital absence of pain was made, which was confirmed by Dr E.A. Carmichael who kindly saw him in consultation at the National Hospital, Queen Square. The parents were given to understand what the condition entailed, particularly for such serious conditions as an acute abdomen or a fractured limb. Supportive counselling was provided by the medical social case worker to help the parents to adjust emotionally to their child's condition.

Nothing untoward occurred till he was 21 months of age, when he was noticed to have a swollen left leg and was seen at the hospital after it had been present for three weeks. A fracture at the lower end of the tibia and fibula was seen on X-ray with excessive callous formation presumably due to unlimited and unrestricted activity. Although this was thought to be healing satisfactorily, an abscess developed two weeks later over the site of the fracture, which turned out to be a discharging sinus from an underlying osteomyelitis necessitating prolonged chemotherapy and hospitalization for almost two months. Since then he has sustained a fracture of a metatarsal which was discovered by X-ray when he was noticed to be walking strangely. Like earlier, there was a complete lack of pain with a good deal of local swelling and thickening.

Summary

This unusual and uncommon condition is well illustrated by the patient described. It is undoubtedly a serious and hazardous disease since the absence of pain with the lack of protective warning when the body is in any way damaged means the tissues may be seriously damaged before being recognized and treatment given. There is no treatment for the disease itself and the management depends on the vigilance of the parents and later of the patient for any untoward bodily happening.

The evolution of pain is interesting. All organisms develop an ability to hunt for food, a violent process that could cause bodily injury. If an organism gets injured, i.e., sustains physical damage, pain acts as a signal to the nervous system. If an organism sustains injury to the nervous system, it usually does not result in pain. Therefore, the pain signal is probably to get the organism to stop moving, since rest is a fundamental and simple response to physical pain. Secondly, pain has an anticipatory value: it teaches the animal to avoid future conditions that may cause pain (and may potentially be life-threatening)—thus improving the overall fitness of the population. The better adapted, or 'fit', an organism is, the more likely the species is to survive. Gene pools of animals 'contribute' genes to future fitness of generations, selectively choosing the genes that give the creature an increased ability to survive and reproduce. Researchers studied the evolution of pain as a measure of fitness, and found that it increased the fitness of a population—it improved a colony's ability to avoid danger, and also to 'manage' bodily illness or injury better.

The nervous system receives many different impulses simultaneously, and the animal has to prioritize which one it responds to. If the sense of touch is critical to our communication and navigation, the sense of pain is essential for survival and adaptation. The perception of pain is called 'nociception'. Just as we discussed thermoreceptors and mechanoreceptors, we now look at receptors involved in pain sensation—nociceptors. These are essentially free nerve endings located in the skin (and below it), and many share pathways with nerves that transmit touch and pressure. While joints and tendons too have nociceptors, they are more numerous in the skin. Interestingly, the brain does not have nociceptors. Why would an organ that ultimately senses pain not have its own pain sensor? Yet, this is strangely logical because if there is an impact that damages the brain, the animal is unlikely to survive anyway.

Nerves are classified into A, B and C fibres, of which A and B fibres are myelinated. (Myelin is the sheath that surrounds nerves, rather like insulation around electric cables; its main advantage is in increasing the transmission speed of impulses.) When a nerve is damaged, the myelin sheath provides the direction in which cells can repair, even if such repairs are often inefficient and unsuccessful.

Type **A** muscle fibres are subdivided into α (involved in position-sense and movement, with a conduction speed of 70–120m/s); β (involved in touch, pressure and also movement, with a conduction speed of 30–70m/s); γ (involved in supplying muscles with a conduction speed of 15–30m/s); and δ (involved in pain, cold and touch sensations, with a velocity of 12–30m/s).

B fibres have no subdivisions and are also myelinated, but they are related to the autonomic system, or involuntary nerves (velocity of 3–15m/s).

C fibres are unmyelinated axons, and these are divided into dorsal root and sympathetic fibres. The dorsal root fibres carry sensations of pain, temperature and mechanoreception, with a velocity of 0.5 to 2m/s. (Sympathetic fibres are also part of the autonomic nervous system, but I won't discuss them further.)

Therefore, three types of neurons (nerve cells) carry pain signals—Aα, Aδ and C fibres. Of these, Aα tend to carry both pain and non-pain stimuli and are, therefore, not pure nociceptors, so I won't detail them further. Aδ and C nerve cells are pure nociceptors, though, so let's look at them more closely.

Aδ fibres are myelinated and about 2–5μm thick, while C fibres are up to 1.5μm thick. These are specialized nociceptors, i.e., specialized to detect noxious stimuli such as pain. Aδ fibres carry sharp or pricking pain—like if you stood on a thorn or needle, or were having a heart attack—and are therefore fast-acting, given their myelin sheaths and fast velocity. C fibres are non-myelinated and usually sense burning or throbbing pain, and are slower-felt than sharp pain. It is important to note that while they transmit different impulses, both fibres share common pain pathways, like sharing routing telecommunication cables. The spinal cord is the origin of these nociceptive fibres, and the thalamus of the brain is where the pain centre is located. That's why these pathways are collectively referred to as the 'spinothalamic tract'.

The lack of Aδ fibres would make pain perception entirely impossible, which of course has serious implications. The absence of C fibres affects pain perception on the skin, given that it shares the nociceptive pathway with Aδ fibres. So, the individual would note the pain, but not think it was significant. Therefore, when it comes to sensing pain from the skin, these Aδ and C fibres find themselves in an uncomfortable union, as Julie Molloy from Manchester discovered when she was in labour. As she could feel no pain, doctors had to monitor her progress and induce her before nightfall because they were worried she'd go into labour at night and not know it. Fortunately, her son Landon was born with all his senses intact.

For Julie, chopping potatoes is a major task; she needs to check she is not holding the knife the wrong way around or if an itinerant finger is in the way, waiting to be chopped off. Julie has hereditary Type II sensory neuropathy, a condition which wipes out all myelinated fibres in affected areas, and as the Aα tend to carry both pain and non-pain stimuli, like touch and pressure, Julie completely lacks these sensations. Unable to feel any sensations on her feet, she was determined to drive, even if she cannot feel the pedals or know where her feet are placed relative to them. She has to glance down to make sure she has her feet on the right pedals. Her family reckons she's a bit hard on the brakes. But determination can make a good driver and Julie passed her driving test easily. These days, she has stumps of calluses on her hands and feet from injuries sustained unknowingly. Her condition has not stopped her from working in a marketing job or raising her son. She hopes for a cure, even if she knows it is unlikely in her lifetime.

Medicine owes a lot to the humble leech. In fact, the word 'leech' in modern English comes from the old English word 'laece', meaning physician. Medicinal leeches have been around for centuries. Treatment using *Hirudo medicinali* leeches has been prescribed for blocked or congested veins (as in thrombophlebitis or haematomas), and even for fluid in joints from arthritis. Avicenna describes such hirudotherapy (the leech derives its name from 'hirudin', a substance in its saliva that inhibits clotting of blood) in his *Canon of Medicine* in 1020. Bloodletting enjoyed favour in medical practice, especially during the time of Napoleon Bonaparte. Francois Joseph Victor Broussais, who served as a military surgeon in Napoleon's army, sometimes applied as many as ten to fifty leeches at a time for certain maladies. A healthy leech was said to draw 'one to two drachms of blood' (drachm is the archaic spelling of 'dram', a term whisky drinkers will be familiar with). An aside here: in the seventeenth-century British Isles, a teaspoon was defined as one fluid dram. In the eighteenth century, the East India Company imported tea directly back to England, and as the price of tea came down, the teaspoon sizes went up to 1/3 tablespoon or one-and-a-half fluid dram (around 5ml).

People observed how wounds still bled awhile after the leech was removed. In 1884, John Berry Haycroft from Birmingham discovered the anticoagulant substance, hirudin, which leeches inject into blood to thin it. This was when people understood the mechanism of Avicenna's treatment, and the term hirudotherapy was coined.

Given their significance, leeches find a place in classical literature and poetry:

> He with a smile did then his words repeat;
> And said that, gathering Leeches, far and wide
> He travelled; stirring thus about his feet
> The waters of the Pools where they abide.
> Once I could meet with them on every side;

But they have dwindled long by slow decay;
Yet still I persevere, and find them where I may.
– William Wordsworth, describing the
'leech-gatherer'[13]

A few years ago, I had to perform a complicated flap operation (where tissue from somewhere else is moved to fill a defect) to reconstruct a lip, because a large portion of it had been affected by skin cancer. One of the risks of flap surgery is venous congestion. What this means is that if there is excessive tension due to the build-up of venous blood, circulation of blood to the flap can be compromised due to the increased pressure, leading to tissue death. In other parts of the body, it is easier to drain blood collections under flaps, but given that the lip is already a bloody cushion, and the complex nature of the flap, we decided to use medicinal leeches (*see plate section*). The suckers of the leech would latch on to the lip until the creature was fully engorged, and it would simply fall off when sated. The resident doctors (and the patient) looked on with a mixture of admiration and horror. The treatment worked. This ancient remedy has made a comeback in the world of medicine, to such an extent that the FDA (US Food and Drug Administration) has now deemed that the humble leech can be classified as a 'medical device'.

However, that isn't the reason I'm bringing this up right now. See, leeches were the first animals to show evidence of having nociceptors or pain receptors. While even primitive organisms communicate by touch, there is no evidence that they had specific sensations of pain, until leeches, that is.

The leech is divided into many segments, and each segment has strikingly similar arrangements of ganglia (bundles of nerves) and temperature (T), pressure (P) and nociceptive (N) receptors. Interestingly, these were specific receptors. Researchers found that P and N cells never respond to light touch, and N cells always need much more pressure than P cells. Are these *skin* nociceptors? Well, if you removed the skin from a leech, none of these sensations occurred.

Remember we discussed ATP in the context of mitochondrial energy production? ATPase is the enzyme that breaks down ATP into ADP and a free, i.e., inorganic, phosphate ion—this hydrolysis of ATP produces energy.

The ATPase enzymes work at the cell membranes, and 'import' substances needed for many functions. In actual fact, there are many different kinds of ATPase enzymes within biological membranes. For example, a H^+/K^+ATPase (hydrogen-potassium ATPase) pump is used in the stomach to make the contents more acidic.

For excitable cells, like nerve cells that need some 'stimulation', a different kind of ATPase pump is activated. This Na^+K^+ATPase (sodium-potassium ATPase) pump is an exchanger: it helps pump three sodium (Na^+) ions out of the cell into extracellular spaces; in exchange, two potassium (K^+) ions enter the cell.

Remember we discussed that thermoregulation in fish used the sodium pump? This is essentially the modulation of the sodium-potassium ATPase pump. There is increasing evidence that the sodium pump, which is present in the cell membranes of all animals, could be what powers synapses between nerves. The sodium pump (*see Figure 32*) was discovered in the 1950s by Jens Skou, a Dane, who was awarded the Nobel Prize in 1997.

It's interesting that leprosy should still have such stigma attached to it. You wouldn't guess that it is one of the least contagious diseases, and that many people have innate immunity to it. Yet, from biblical times, leprosy and lepers have been treated as outcastes. Around 2,500 years ago, the Nile Valley considered leprosy incurable. It was during their return from Palestine that the Crusaders brought leprosy to Europe, leading to an epidemic in Britain around AD 1000 to 1200. This was when the first leper-houses were built in England.

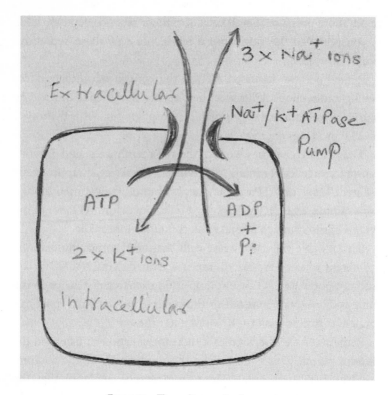

FIGURE 32   The sodium–potassium pump

Around AD 1100 in England, legal enactments prohibited lepers from leaving their assigned homes, making wills or inheriting property. In other words, lepers were 'worse than dead' in the eyes of the law.

In the late 1890s in England, lepers received free board and lodging, and were spared many duties that were compulsory for other citizens. They also had a 'right to beg', which led many people to falsely claim their 'leprosy benefit' and that in turn elevated the disease statistics in England, causing leprosy to appear more prevalent than it actually was.

We've all read about Father Damien, the Belgian priest who came to the island of Molokai in Hawaii in 1864, and later dedicated his life to the leper colony in Kalakaua. The story goes that, after about

20 years, when he accidentally spilt boiling water on his feet and could not feel a thing, Father Damien knew that the disease had caught up with him. It is worth studying this biology of nerve injury in leprosy and how it affects skin sensations, given that leprosy is the best known amongst diseases that affect sensations of skin (even if diabetes is now becoming the commonest cause of nerve damage). *Mycobacterium leprae*, which is the pathogen in leprosy, localizes in the nerves and causes an inflammatory process. It was initially thought that the mycobacterium first attached itself to Schwann cells (*see Figure 28*) that surround the axon and then moved higher up the nerve, 'like swimming upstream'.

This explanation, while elegant, was not accurate, as it did not explain how an essentially non-motile mycobacterium could jump between the internodes that separated Schwann cells. Researchers now feel that leprosy causes demyelination (loss of the myelin sheath, which may be a result of inflammation of the nerves), axonal injury and an antibody response. Contrary to popular belief, leprosy does not cause fingers or limbs to fall off; it is the lack of sensation because of nerve demyelination and inflammation that causes injuries, which in turn lead to repeated infections. If left untreated, the neuritis can travel deeper in the body and affect the eyes.

Researchers at Rockefeller University identified a component on the surface of the bacterium that specifically selects nerves on the skin. The cell wall of *Mycobacterium leprae* has a glycolipid called PGL-1 (phenolic glycolipid-1). Cell wall glycolipids and sugars are especially important for cell and target identification, and many bacteria communicate using these 'secret handshakes'. In leprosy, basal lamina and Schwann cells respond to PGL-1 upon contact with the bacterium by opening a pathway for the intruder to enter and cause inflammation and nerve damage.

In the early 1990s, Paul Brand, the celebrated orthopaedic and hand surgeon who worked as a missionary surgeon in the field of leprosy, wrote a book called *Pain: The Gift Nobody Wants*.[14] Brand had spent many years in India perfecting tendon transfer techniques—surgical methods that were invaluable in helping severely deformed hands become more able—and had come to realize that a life without pain is dangerous, even miserable. After all, in leprosy, the fundamental problem is that the skin sensations of pain were diminished, leading to injury. Brand wrote:

> We dare not allow our daily lives to become so comfortable that we are no longer challenged to grow, to seek adventure, to risk … Lasting pleasure is more apt to come as a surprising bonus from something I have invested myself in. Most likely that investment will include pain—it's hard to imagine pleasure without it.

Paul Brand spent many years as a medical missionary at the Christian Medical College in Vellore, Tamil Nadu. There is a slight family connection here. Both my parents studied medicine there and went on to medical mission work; my father, now retired from surgical practice, once worked with Paul Brand.

Notes

1. Jeanette Winterson, *Written on the Body*, Vintage, 1994.
2. Aristotle, *Metaphysics*, Book 1, Section 980a, 21, http://www.perseus.tufts.edu/hopper/text?doc=urn:cts:greekLit:tlg0086.tlg025.perseus-eng1:1.980a, accessed 17 March 2012.
3. Aristotle (c. 350 BC), translated by J. A. Smith, *De Anima* (On the Soul), An Internet resource developed by Christopher D. Green, York University, Toronto, Ontario, http://psychclassics.yorku.ca/Aristotle/De-anima/, accessed 17 March 2012.
4. Constance Classen, 'Fingerprints: Writing About Touch', in *The Book of Touch: Sensory Formations Series*, Concordia University, July 2005, p. 1.
5. Jonathan Bennett, *Locke, Berkeley, Hume: Central Themes*, Oxford University Press, Oxford, 1971, p. 102.
6. Charles Darwin, *The Power of Movement in Plants*, John Murray, London, 1880, p. 573.
7. John S. Tuckey (Ed.), *The Devil's Race-Track: Mark Twain's Great Dark Writings*, Berkeley: University of California Press, 1980, p. 340–41.
8. Arthur Weissmann, 'Friedrich Sigmund Merkel: Part 1: The Man', *The*

American Journal of Dermatopathology, Vol. 4, No. 6, December 1982, pp. 521–26.

9. Arthur Weissmann, 'Friedrich Sigmund Merkel: Part II: The Cell', *The American Journal of Dermatopathology*, Vol. 4, No. 6, December 1982, pp. 521–26.

10. atonal: lacking tone or key, (n.d.) *The American Heritage® Dictionary of the English Language*, 4th ed., 2003, http://www.thefreedictionary.com/atonal, accessed on 17 March 2012.

11. From 'God', *John Lennon/Plastic Ono Band*.

12. David Morris, 'Congenital Absence of Pain', *Postgraduate Medical Journal*, November 1962, p. 641.

13. 'Resolution and Independence,' by William Wordsworth, reproduced in Charles W. Eliot (ed.), *English Poetry II: From Collins to Fitzgerald*, Vol. XLI, The Harvard Classics Series, P.F. Collier & Son, 1909–14, New York, www.bartleby.com/41/, accessed 17 March 2012.

14. Paul Brand and Philip Yancy, (later retitled) *The Gift of Pain*, Zondervan Press, 1997, p. 301.

TEN

Technology vs Natural Order

I mean, our ancestors, two or three million years ago, you
know, would probably be quite upset if they could realize,
you know, they would become extinct and lead to us. The
computers are probably our successors, the intelligent
computers of the future ... I only hope that they'll—if you're
still around—they'll treat us kindly like household pets.

– Arthur C. Clarke[1]

I've mentioned earlier that on Fridays I teach creative writing to
disadvantaged school children. The kids know that I work in the
field of skin cancer and surgery, and often ask about my work and
to see photos from my reconstructive surgery archives—the gorier
the better!

'What do you think skin does?' I asked a class one day.

'It gives the body some shape,' a little boy called out.

Most people think that skin gives body tissues its shape, that if
you removed skin, you'd rip open a body like an envelope, and the
innards would fall out in one unholy mess. But that function, of
maintaining structure, is actually the domain of fascia—which is the
layer of connective or fibrous tissue that surrounds muscles, nerves,
blood vessels, binding the whole together.

The dermis is the deeper layer of skin. This layer is responsible for
maintaining the shape of our skin (just as fascia maintains the shape

of our body), as it contains collagen fibres and also sweat glands, oil glands, hair follicles and blood vessels.

The dermis contains fibroblast cells that produce collagen. Thin collagen bundles are located in its upper layer (papillary dermis), and thick parallel bundles of collagen in its deeper layer (reticular dermis). When an injury is deep enough to involve the dermis, fibroblasts from the surrounding areas also start producing collagen to fill the injured area. This is a lot like manufacturing cement to fill a wall that has been breached or damaged.

There are two types of fibres produced by the fibroblasts of the dermis. Collagen is responsible for the firmness and plumpness of skin, and loss of collagen can make skin appear loose and wrinkled. Elastin affects elasticity, i.e., the ability of skin to return to its shape when pinched. Brown skin, provided there is no dehydration or malnutrition, does not wrinkle easily. As a young man said to me in New York: 'Black don't crack.' However, just like dark-skinned epidermal cells contain larger melanosomes, fibroblasts in the brown skin type are larger. This is the reason why brown-skinned patients or Asian patients scar more easily and why laser surgery, which often gives good results in white skin, may not give brown skin the same results.

Speaking of skin colours, we noted earlier that the skin's outer layer, epidermis, is what gives us our colour through the distribution of melanocytes, which are found in its basal layer and also in the matrix of hair bulbs. As we discussed earlier, 'eumelanin' is the brown-black melanin found in brown skin types; 'pheomelanin' is red-yellow melanin found in people with red hair. However, there are other colours that affect skin tone and shades. Haemoglobin from arteries appears red as it carries oxygen, and is blue in the veins as it returns blood to the lungs for oxygen supply. Our bodies also contain caroteinoids, which are found in food sources like carrots and many other vegetables. These are taken up by the body and all these red, blue and yellow pigments mix to form different shades of skin tone.

Most of my initial plastic surgery work was in the field of burns and trauma before I specialized in skin cancer. One of the problems of dealing with patients with large parts of their bodies burnt is that, without the skin's protective effect, the body loses metabolites and becomes dehydrated. This, in turn, makes the burnt skin vulnerable to infections.

There was always some explanation or the other, but in my days as a plastic surgery resident in India more than two decades ago, the typical burn victim would be young, female, recently married, more often from north India, with the family claiming it was a kitchen accident. One or two of the young women managed to tell us the horrible truth before they died. The other resident doctors and I were enraged because most of these 'accidental' burn victims had obviously been burnt alive for failing to meet their in-laws' increasing demands for dowry. We were frustrated that there was very little we could do when more than 50 per cent of the skin surface area was burnt. This is because the extensive skin loss causes loss of electrolytes and fluids to an extent incompatible with normal body function.

In treating burns, we normally treat full thickness skin loss— when both epidermis and dermis have been lost—by grafting partial-thickness (skin containing epidermis and only a portion of dermis) skin taken from another part of the patient's body (the halo graft I've invented is also a type of partial-thickness skin graft, which is useful after removal of skin cancers, especially on the leg).

Obviously, in burn victims, the donor site (where the skin was taken from) is also at risk of infection as the epidermal enclosure no longer exists. The fact that the donor site then produces an epidermis means that the dermis somehow sends cellular information, which then coordinates the healing and regeneration process.

It follows then that if we were to design an artificial skin, we'd need the dermis to still be able to modulate the healing process and stimulate new epidermal growth. This was a dilemma for researchers: what synthetic polymer could handle the complex functions of skin?

> For when his day's work is done his business more properly begins
> For he keeps the Lord's watch in the night against the adversary
> For he counteracts the powers of darkness by his electrical skin …
>
> — Jubliate Agno[2]

John Francis Burke was born in 1922 in Illinois. He was studying chemical engineering at the University of Illinois when World War II broke out. A day after the Pearl Harbour attack, he joined the army and decided to become a psychiatrist because he felt the military did very little for 'men with emotional troubles'. After receiving a bachelor's degree at Illinois in 1947, he went to Harvard and decided to become a surgeon.

John Burke felt that, as a plastic surgeon, he understood skin biology. But his chemical engineering education told him that he needed mechanical engineering expertise to solve the problem of an artificial dermis. He went to Ioannis Yannas, a professor of fibres and polymers at MIT, with his specifications and design considerations for human skin. Eleven years later, the duo came up with a combination of plastics, cow tissue and shark cartilage—a commercially manufactured artificial skin that had two layers.

The top layer, an artificial epidermis, was essentially a silicone sheet that prevented infection and dehydration; the lower layer, the artificial dermis, was a scaffold made of molecular material from cow tendons and shark cartilage. What was amazing was that this acted as a seed, and healthy skin cells grew into the scaffolding within a month. Eventually, the shark and cow tissues were completely absorbed by the human body. The upper silicone layer was then peeled off and the skin was allowed to heal like an abrasion. The artificial skin saved hundreds of lives.

Leonardo Da Vinci once wrote:[3]

> Though human ingenuity may make various inventions which, by the help of various machines answering the same end, it will never

devise any inventions more beautiful, nor more simple, nor more to the purpose than Nature does; because in her inventions nothing is wanting, and nothing is superfluous, and she needs no counterpoise when she makes limbs proper for motion in the bodies of animals. But she puts into them the soul of the body, which forms them that is the soul of the mother which first constructs in the womb the form of the man and in due time awakens the soul that is to inhabit it.

As we've seen, skin essentially keeps us hydrated, forms a blockade against foreign bacteria and UV radiation, serves as a sensory organ and cools us with sweat. However, this last task proved to be too complex for modern technology to master. Artificial skin had no sweat glands, and therefore its recipients could not undertake vigorous exercise due to the risk that the body would overheat. It was with the creation of human-made skin that we fully realized the importance of skin as a thermoregulatory organ, and the importance of sweat in the scheme of things. Scientists were rudely reminded of the limits of technology. Nature was not going to let thousands of years of evolution be reproduced without a nod to its meticulousness. Skin understands this—in the ultimate analysis, it isn't about right or wrong, but an acceptance that things are so …

It is sobering to think that what nature can create so effortlessly, all our technology cannot. However, Dr John Burke, a pioneer in the development of artificial skin, was the first to come audaciously close. Dr Burke had come to the realization that the fundamental fact of human biology was the communication between different bodily parts and organs; what he and Yannas had accomplished was the creation of a synthetic material that could also interact with the patient, and stimulate the right kind of cells to do the needful things.[4]

One of the challenges for doctors when performing an internal examination is that, while the gloved fingertips can feel possible tumours or feel the prostate or cervix, they cannot discern much more detail. To overcome this, researchers have developed 'smart gloves'—essentially, ultra-thin; stretchable, silicon-based electronics and soft sensors attached to gloves made of 'silicon skin' and fitted to fingertips. In the future, this technology can help detect electrical properties of tissue or help surgeons perform ultrasound scans while examining patients. It may even save diabetics from having to prick their fingertips for blood glucose testing.

In the 1970s, scientists discovered that they could alter an animal's genetic make-up. They found they could literally 'cut' a gene out using chemical scissors and 'paste' the cut fragment. Let's say you wanted to make more insulin: you first cut (using a restriction enzyme) the plasmid out of an E. coli bacterium and then paste it in insulin-making human DNA. (Plasmid is a DNA molecule that is separate from, and can reproduce independent of, chromosomal DNA. These are double-stranded and, in many cases, circular.) The resulting hybrid plasmid can be inserted into another E. coli bacterium, where it multiplies along with the bacterium. There, it can produce large quantities of insulin because E. coli can reproduce voraciously.

As we have seen, scientists use model organisms like the fruit fly or E.coli to study genetics and genetic engineering. This raised a question: instead of using stem cells to create skin, what about using skin cells to create stem cells? After all, skin cells replicate easily and constantly produce more cells, making them ideal cell generators. This seemingly topsy-turvy idea, it turns out, works pretty well. On 21 November 2007, Japanese professor Shinya Yamanaka published his breakthrough in direct 'reprogramming': creating the equivalent of cloned embryonic stem cells from adult skin cells, never using women's eggs and never creating or destroying embryos. Essentially, Professor Yamanuka and his colleagues used a retrovirus to 'ferry' into adult cells the same four genes they had previously used to reprogram mouse cells. This resulted in human skin cells producing stem cells. These cells can be used to regrow nerves or other tissue because they are pluripotent, i.e., capable of developing into other tissues.

Stem cells in general regulate tissue replacement. In the skin, they are responsible for overseeing the keratinocyte factory. During the day, skin is exposed to UV radiation from the sun, and when we are at work, we are constantly exposed to bacteria and viruses. Research now shows that these stem cells may be regulated by our body's biological clock, which ensures that the stem cells divide when the body is not exposed to UV radiation—at night, for instance. By ensuring that the stem cell factory production lines run during periods of low risk and low exposure to infections, production quality is better and tumour risk is lower.

People who have been opposed to stem cell research from human embryos rejoiced, as this new technique of using skin cells eliminated the need for using human embryos. Dr Mehmet Oz, on an Oprah Winfrey Show that featured actor Michael J. Fox and discussed the benefits of using skin stem cells in research into Parkinson's disease, said:[5]

> I think, Oprah, the stem cell debate is dead, and I'll tell you why ...
> The problem with embryonic stem cells is that they come from embryos, like all of us were made from embryos ... In the last year we've made ten years' advancement ... and here's what the deal is: I can take a little bit of your skin, take those cells, and get them to go back in time so they're like they were when you were first made.

However, it is easy to forget in our excitement that we are essentially using a retrovirus to produce other stem cells from skin cells, the same kind of virus that causes AIDS. Many scientists fear that these viruses could trigger tumours or disease in tissues produced by this technique.

Einstein once warned: 'Technological progress is like an axe in the hands of a pathological criminal.'[6]

The discovery that tissues from other animals can be used to create new polymers has led to recent experiments with spiderweb. This is because spiderwebs are pound-for-pound the strongest material known to mankind, and researchers have long been trying to harness this knowledge.

Recently, a Utah researcher, Randy Lewis, inserted spider genes into goats and silkworms to create 'spider silk'. Spider silk is more than five times as strong as steel. This aroused the curiosity of Dutch artist Jalila Essaidi, who created a lattice of artificial skin using this spider silk. Essaidi, who demonstrated her project at the Designers & Artists 4 Genomics Awards, initially thought Lewis's spider silk from goats would capture the 'grotesque factor' of the mammal–spider combination. Using a high-speed camera, she conducted an experiment. A bullet was fired at a lower speed at Lewis's genetically engineered worm's silk that had been 'grafted' between the epidermis and dermis. The skin *didn't* break. She had stumbled upon 'bullet-proof' skin. One can already imagine the military applications of this bullet-proof skin in the not-too-distant future. She has been quoted as saying:[7]

> I want to explore the social, political, ethical and cultural issues surrounding safety in a world with access to new biotechnologies.
> It is legend that Achilles was invulnerable in all of his body except for his heel. Will we in the near future no longer need to descend from a godly bloodline in order to have traits like invulnerability?

And speaking of fashionable uses for synthetic skin, the manufacturers of SkinBag,[8] a synthetic skin composed of silicone, polyurethane and rubber—similar to the artificial skin used in burns—have this to say: 'SkinBag is a synthetic skin recognizable by its wrinkled texture and organic appearance; available in all colours, including two-toned for some membranes. It is also possible to personalize the texture with "scarifications" such as inscriptions or drawings.'

You can even ask for specific placements of veins or scars on your skin clothing. Bizarre or not, Oliver Goulet of SkinBag has just released a range of his designer jackets (*see plate section*) made of this synthetic skin.[9] I'm on my way to try one for size!

I've just discussed how modern technology has attempted to recreate skin for medical, military, artistic and technological purposes, but what about the natural order of skin?

Stephen Greenblatt has written a masterful historical book on the Renaissance period, titled *The Swerve*,[10] essentially dissecting Lucretius's famous poem, which says that nothing can violate the laws of nature, and everything is a result of random collisions of particles that often cause a change of direction, a *clinamen*, which Greenblatt translates as 'swerve'.

When I was at university, I tried to read Copley's translation of this *De rerum natura* (On the Nature of Things),[11] which was written in verse by Titus Lucretius Carus (whom we know as the Roman, Lucretius), around 50 BC, in an attempt to explain Epicurus's teachings to a wider audience. Epicurus held remarkably modern views: that humans did not hold a special place that set them above animals, there was no hope in bribing gods to appease them, no place for religious fanaticism or wars of conquest, and that no possibility existed of attaining complete security or triumph over nature. He believed that the entire universe was random and made up anatomically of atoms. Species are created by natural selection and die if incompatible with the environment. Ultimately, no species, planet or star is immortal; only atoms are.

With apologies to Lucretius and Epicurus, I've come up with my own laws—*de natura cutis* (On the Nature of Skin):

1. Skin cells are infinite in number, but limited by size and shape individually.
2. Skin cells are constantly renewed and repaired.
3. Skin has no maker or designer, but allows nature to experiment ceaselessly.
4. Skin didn't evolve for humans alone, which is why it is a universal organ and many creatures share the genes that regulate skin development.
5. Skin was born at an early time when oceans were shallow and

particles in random motion collided to create the beginnings of life itself.

6. Skin colours were formed due to constant competition between two vitamins when exposed to the sun.

7. The greatest endowments that skin offers are to do with the pleasure of touch and the gift of pain.

8. Understanding the commonality of skin, the organ, is key to being comfortable in one's own skin.

9. Ultimately, no species or organ has survived the test of time; *only* skin has. This fact alone must make us appreciate the greatness of the biography of skin.

As William Shakespeare wrote (*Troilus and Cressida* , Act III, Scene iii): One touch of nature makes the whole world kin.

NOTES

1. Interview: 'Science Fiction Author Arthur C. Clarke on New Millennium Predictions', National Public Radio, Washington, DC, 1999.

2. Jubliate Agno (c. 1758-63) Fragment B, L 719.

3. *The Notebooks of Leonardo Da Vinci*, p. 27, http://italian.classic-literature.co.uk/leonardo-da-vinci/book-page-26.asp, accessed 17 March 2012.

4. Paul Vitello, 'Dr. John F. Burke, Dies at 89; Created Synthetic Skin', *The New York Times*, 5 November 2011, http://www.nytimes.com/2011/11/06/us/dr-john-f-burke-dies-at-89-created-synthetic-skin.html, accessed 17 March 2012.

5. Dr Mehmet Oz on the Oprah Winfrey Show, featuring Dr Oz and Michael J. Fox, 31 March 2009.

6. From http://www.einstein-quotes.com/Science.html, accessed 17 March 2012.

7. 'Utah researcher helps artist make bulletproof skin', AP foreign news, *The Guardian*, Wednesday, 24 August 2011.

8. Organic objects in synthetic skin, http://www.skinbag.net/, accessed 17 March 2012.

9. Iain Hutchison, 'Celebrating skin', *The Lancet*, Vol. 376; No. 9736, 17–23 July 2010, pp. 156–57.

10. Stephen Greenblatt, *The Swerve—how the Renaissance began*, Vintage Books, London, 2012.
11. Frank O. Copley translation, *The Nature of Things*, W.W. Norton & Company, New York, 1977.

Afterword

It is sometimes said that the best works are those that are written inside-out—if you want to write about mountains, don't observe them, but climb them; if you want to write about rivers, row them. When I first began to ponder this biography of skin, I realized I needed to write from 'the inside'. Not just my medical patient histories, but of the sometimes ambiguous development of this illimitable organ, to the way it changed colour several times—minuscule genetic changes moderated by nothing other than a process of trial and error—each machination leading to another small visible change, yet not one of these alterations privileged over others, except in the eyes of biased beholders.

Research in this case became like art or writing fiction, where the process was as important as the finished work, and I gradually acquired new skills and ideas along the way—a bit like the birth, development and life of skin itself. Skin might have had its doubts, just as I did.

But now this organ knows the wondrousness of its own story, just as I think I understand it better. As I run my fingers over my arm and feel the texture of evolutionary perfection, I have also come to the conclusion that skin is interesting to me and other people because it is sufficiently changeable and unpredictable enough to be mysterious and attractive. Neither a doctor nor a philosopher can completely understand it, although they can explore its infiniteness. Skin has become both the master of our destiny and appearance.

It is night as I finish writing this book. I get into bed and feel the warmth of the bed sheets. I feel a thin layer of sweat on my skin and pull back the outer blanket. As I sit up to do this, through the slit in the curtain I can see a ghosted street light. My phone rings almost simultaneously and I hear a muffled, throaty voice: *Dr Paul, this is regarding my skin cancer operation …*

References

CHAPTER 1

1. John O'Donohue, *Anam Cara: A Book of Celtic Wisdom*, HarperCollins, 1998.

2. Aranzazu Amor, Ana Enríquez, 'Is infection by *Dermatophilus congolensis* underdiagnosed?', *J. Clinical. Microbiology*, January 2011, Vol. 49, No. 1, pp. 449–51.

3. Joanna Robinson, 'Skin Deep', *River Teeth: A Journal of Nonfiction Narrative*, Vol. 9, No. 1, Fall 2007, pp. 36–41.

4. E. Arens and H. Zhang, 'The Skin's Role in Human Thermoregulation and Comfort', *Thermal and Moisture Transport in Fibrous Materials*, Eds N. Pan and P. Gibson, Woodhead Publishing Ltd, 2006, pp. 560–602.

5. Shashidhar Kusuma, Ravi K. Vuthoori, Melissa Piliang, and James E. Zins, 'Skin anatomy and physiology', *Plastic and Reconstructive Surgery*, Ed. Maria Z. Siemionow, Springer, 2010, pp. 161–71.

6. Madhu A. Pathak, 'In memory of Thomas Bernhard Fitzpatrick', *Journal of Investigative Dermatology*, 2004, p. 122.

7. T.B. Fitzpatrick, 'The validity and practicality of sun-reactive skin types I through VI', *Archives of Dermatology*, June 1988, 124(6), pp. 869–71.

Chapter 2

1. Darwin to Gray (22 May 1860) LLD, II:311–2; CCD, VIII:224; Darwin to Gray (26 Nov 1860) LLD, II:353–4; and CCD, VIII:496. Sourced from Denis O. Lamoureux, *Theological Insights from Charles Darwin*, http://www.asa3.org/ASA/PSCF/2004/PSCF3-04Lamoureux.pdf, accessed 12 March 2012.

2. Nicholas Wade, 'Stanley Miller, Who Examined Origins of Life, Dies at 77', *The New York Times*, 23 May 2007.

3. Stanley L. Miller, 'A production of amino acids under possible primitive earth conditions', *Science*, New Series, Vol. 117, No. 3046, 15 May 1953, pp. 528–29.

4. N.C. Wickramasinghe and F. Hoyle, 'Miller–Urey synthesis in the nuclei of galaxies', *Astrophysics and Space Science*, 259: 1988, pp. 99–103.

5. John Matson, 'Meteorite that fell in 1969 still revealing secrets of the early solar system', *Scientific American*, 15 February 2010.

6. Laurence Marshall, 'Conflict in the cosmos: Fred Hoyle's life', *Science Natural History*, Vol. 114, No. 8, October 2005, p. 60.

7. Press Release, 'The 1989 Nobel Prize in Chemistry', 5 December 2011, http://www.nobelprize.org/nobel_prizes/chemistry/laureates/1989/press.html, accessed 12 March 2012.

8. S. Pizzarello & A.L. Weber, 'Prebiotic amino acids as asymmetric catalysts', *Science*, 20 February 2004, 303 (5661), p. 1151.

9. Charles Darwin letter, as quoted in: J.D. Bernal, *The Origin of Life*, Weidenfeld and Nicholson, 1967, London.

10. 'RNA and DNA Revealed: New Roles, New Rules', *The New Genetics*, NIH National Institute of General Medical Science, http://publications.nigms.nih.gov/thenewgenetics/chapter2.html, accessed 17 March 2012.

11. Karen Bernardo, 'Characterization in Literature', http://learn.lexiconic.net/characters.htm, accessed 17 March 2012.

12. P. Forterre, J. Filée, H. Myllykallio, 'Origin and evolution of DNA and DNA replication machineries', Madame Curie Bioscience Database, Austin (TX), Landes Bioscience, 2000–, http://www.ncbi.nlm.nih.gov/books/NBK6360/, accessed 17 March 2012.

13. Thomas Jenuwein and C. David Allis, 'Translating the histone code', *Science*, 10 August 2001: Vol. 293, No. 5532, pp. 1074–80.

14. J.L Marx, 'Is RNA copied into DNA by mammalian cells?', *Science*, 28 May 1982, pp. 969–70.

15. '"Accelerated Evolution" Converts RNA Enzyme to DNA Enzyme In Vitro', *ScienceDaily*, 27 March 2006, http://www.sciencedaily.com/releases/2006/03/060327083737.htm, accessed 17 March 2012.

16. Ramachandra Guha, *India After Gandhi: The History of the World's Largest Democracy*, Pan Macmillan, 2008, pp. 769–70.

17. J.B.S. Haldane, 'Data Needed for a Blueprint of the First Organism', in Sidney W. Fox (ed.), *The Origins of Prebiological Systems and of Their Molecular Matrices: Proceedings of a Conference Conducted at Wakulla Springs, Florida, 27–30 October 1963*, Academic Press, New York, 1965, p. 12.

18. Dr Oscar Levy (ed.), *The Complete Works of Friedrich Nietzsche: The First Complete and Authorised English Translation*, Vol. 10 (The Joyful Wisdom; La Gaya Scienza), The Macmillan Company, New York, 1924.

19. Richard Michod et al., 'Life-history evolution and the origin of multicellularity', *Journal of Theoretical Biology*, 239 (2006), pp. 257–72.

21. Nicole King, 'The unicellular ancestry of animal development', *Developmental Cell*, Vol. 7 (2004), pp. 313–25.

22. 'Sponge genome goes deep', *Nature*, published online, 4 August 2010, 466, 673 (2010).

23. 'Skin was the first organ to evolve', *New Scientist*, Issue 2790, 16 December 2010.

24. Ed Regis, *What Is Life: Investigating the Nature of Life in the Age of Synthetic Biology*, Oxford University Press, 2008, p. 114.

25. Stephen M. Barr, 'Miracle of Evolution', http://www.columbia.edu/cu/augustine/2006spring/barr_ft.pdf, accessed 12 March 2012.

26. Mansi Srivastava et al., 'The Amphimedon Queenslandica genome and the evolution of animal complexity', *Nature*, 466, 5 August 2010, pp. 720–26.

27. Nicole King et al., 'The genome of the choanoflagellate *Monosiga brevicollis* and the origin of metazoans, *Nature*, 451, 14 February 2008, pp. 783–88.

CHAPTER 3

1. Jerry Coyne, 'Swatting attacks on fruit flies and science', *The Philadelphia Inquirer*, 31 October 2008; http://richarddawkins.net/articles/3293, accessed 17 March 2012.
2. Elaine Fuchs, 'Scratching the Surface of Skin Development', *Nature*, 445, 22 February 2007, pp. 834–42.
3. Mathew Moore, 'Sonic the Hedgehog voted favourite computer game star', *The Telegraph*, 21 October 2008, website accessed 17 March 2012.
4. Anna Saran, 'Basal cell carcinoma and the carcinogenic role of aberrant hedgehog signalling', *Future Oncology*, 2010; 6(6), pp. 1003–14.
5. Anna Penman, 'The Sonic Hedgehog gene', *The Guardian*, 26 October 2011, website accessed 17 March 2012.
6. 'Roving "Sonic Hedgehog" gene may change scientists' understanding of limb growth', *University of Florida News*, 9 March 2010, http://news.ufl.edu/2010/03/09/sonic/, accessed 17 March 2012.
7. N. Andrews, A.R. Kinsella et al., 'Expression of the E-cadherin–catenin cell adhesion complex in primary squamous cell carcinomas of the head and neck and their nodal metastases', *British Journal of Cancer*, 1997; 75(10), pp. 1474–80.
8. Lewis Wolpert, 'Positional information and the spatial pattern of cellular differentiation', *Journal of Theoretical Biology*, Vol. 25, No. 1, October 1969, pp. 1–47.

CHAPTER 4

1. Charles F. Bennett Jr, 'A review of "Island Life: A Natural History of the Islands of the World" by Sherwin Carlquist', *Geographical Review*, Vol. 56, No. 4 (October 1966), pp. 612–13.
2. Philip D. Gingerich, 'The whales of Tethys', *Natural History*, http://personal.umich.edu/~gingeric/PDFfiles/PDG272_WhalesTethys.pdf, accessed 17 March 2012.
3. Spearman, 'The epidermal stratum corneum of the whale', *J. Anat.* (1972) 113, 3, pp. 373–81.
4. C. Knospe, 'The adaptation to water of whale skin: Histologic and histochemical studies of the dolphin, *Delphinus delphis*, and the porpoise, *Phocaena phocaena*', *Anatomia Histologia Embryologia*, (1989) Volume 18, No. 3, pp. 193–98.

5. Lindsay O'Reilly, 'Kalugsuak's origins: To the Inuit, the Greenland shark holds a place of honour and mystery', *Canadian Geographic*, May 2004, http://www.canadiangeographic.ca/magazine/ma04/indepth/anthropology.asp, accessed 17 March 2012.

6. Kevin N. Laland, John Odling-Smee and Sean Myle, 'How culture shaped the human genome: Bringing genetics and the human sciences together', *Nature Reviews Genetics*, 11, February 2010, pp. 137–48.

CHAPTER 5

1. Nina G. Jablonski and George Chaplin, 'The evolution of human skin coloration', *Journal of Human Evolution*, (2000) 39, pp. 57–106.

2. Gina Kitchener, 'The biology of ... skin color', *Discover Magazine*, published online 1 February 2001, http://discovermagazine.com/2001/feb/featbiology, accessed 17 March 2012.

3. Charles Darwin, *Descent of Man*, D. Appleton and Company, 1871.

4. Toelken Barre, 'The Moccasin Telegraph and Other Improbabilities: A Personal Essay', in *Out of the Ordinary: Folklore and the Supernatural*, Barbara Walker (ed.), Logan: Utah State University Press, 1995, pp. 46–58.

5. Colleen E. Boyd, 'You see your culture coming out of the ground like a power: Uncanny narratives in time and space on the Northwest Coast', *Ethnohistory*, Vol. 56, No. 4, pp. 699–731.

6. Wiete Westerhof, 'Evolutionary, biologic, and social aspects of skin color', *Dermatologic Clinics*, Vol. 25, No. 3, pp. 293–302.

7. Morgan, Elaine, *The Aquatic Ape*, Stein & Day, 1982.

8. Bettina Kujawa, 'Adaptive aspects of hominisation: Locomotion, manipulation and thermoregulation', *Variability and Evolution*, 1996, Vol. 5: pp. 29–42.

9. Martine Luxwolda, 'Traditionally living populations in East Africa have a mean serum 25-hydroxyvitamin D concentration of 115 nmol/l', *British Journal of Nutrition*/FirstView Article, August 2012, pp. 1–5.

10. Antony King, 'Wired society may need vitamin D fortification', *Cosmos* magazine, 12 February 2012, http://www.cosmosmagazine.com/news/5284/traditional-living-provides-more-vitamin-d, accessed 17 March 2012.

Chapter 6

1. 'The murder of Sir Thomas Overbury', *The British Medical Journal*, Vol. 1, No. 3294 (16 February 1924), p. 284.

2. Deepa Joshi (India) and Ben Fawcett (UK), 'Water, Hindu Mythology and an Unequal Social Order in India', Paper presented at the Second Conference of the International Water History Association, Bergen, August 2001.

3. Reetika Vazirani, 'Skin', *Callaloo*, Vol. 27, No. 2 (Spring, 2004), The Johns Hopkins University Press, p. 370.

4. R.A. Sturm, N.F. Box and M. Ramsay, 'Human pigmentation genetics: The difference is only skin deep', *Bioessays*, September 1998, 20(9), pp. 712–21.

5. John David Smith, 'W.E.B. Du Bois, Felix von Luschan, and racial reform at the fin de siècle', *European American Studies*, Vol. 47, No. 1, 2002, pp. 23–38.

6. P. Kerim Friedman, 'Racial differences in skin-colour as recorded by the colour top,' 6 August 2011, http://savageminds.org/2011/08/06/racial-differences-in-skin-colour-as-recorded-by-the-colour-top/, accessed 17 March 2012.

7. Beatrice Blackwood, 'Racial differences in skin-colour as recorded by the colour top', *Journal of the Royal Anthropological Institute of Great Britain and Ireland*, Vol. 60, January–June 1930, pp. 137–68.

8. H.A. Bischoff-Ferrari, W.C. Willett, J.B. Wong, E. Giovannucci, T. Dietrich, B. Dawson-Hughes, 'Fracture prevention with Vitamin D supplementation: A meta-analysis of randomized controlled trials', *Journal of the American Medical Association*, 293:2005, pp. 2257–64.

9. R.P. Heaney, 'Long-latency deficiency disease: Insights from calcium and Vitamin D', *American Journal Clinical Nutrition*, 78:2003, pp. 912–19.

10. Andrew C. Allan, 'MYB transcription factors that colour our fruit', *Trends in Plant Science*, Vol. 13, No. 3, March 2008, pp. 99–102.

11. Richard V. Espley, 'Red colouration in apple fruit is due to the activity of the MYB transcription factor, MdMYB10', *Plant Journal*, 1 February 2007; 49(3), pp. 414–27.

12. A.M. Takos, 'Light-induced expression of a MYB gene regulates anthocyanin biosynthesis in red apples', *Plant Physiology*, 142 (2006), pp. 1216–32.

13. Daniel H. Pink, 'Skin Literature', *The New York Times* magazine, 12 December 2004, http://www.nytimes.com/2004/12/12/magazine/12SKIN.html accessed 17 March 2012.

CHAPTER 7

1. Richard Gooding, 'The Trashing of John McCain', *Vanity Fair*, November 2004, http://www.vanityfair.com/politics/features/2004/11/mccain200411, accessed 17 March 2012.

2. James Schwartz, *In Pursuit of the Gene: from Darwin to DNA*, Harvard University Press, Cambridge, Massachusetts, and London, 2008.

3. Joanne E. Snow, 'Mathematician as Artist', *The Mathematical Intelligencer*, Vol. 32, No. 2, 11–18.

4. Robin Marantz Henig, *The Monk in the Garden: The Lost and Found Genius of Gregor Mendel, the Father of Genetics*, Houghton Mifflin Harcourt, May 2000.

5. Gregor Mendel, 'Experiments in Plant Hybridisation', translated by William Bateson, read at the Natural History Society of Brno Meetings of 8 February and 8 March 1865.

6. Loren Cordain. 'Cereal grains: Humanity's double edged sword', *World Rev Nutr Diet* 1999; 84:19–73.

7. Barry Starr, 'Human Skin Color and Fish Genes—Europeans, East Asians, and Stickleback Fish Became Lighter Because of the Kit Ligand Gene', *The Tech Museum*, Stanford School of Medicine, http://www.thetech.org/genetics/news.php?id=72, accessed 17 March 2012.

8. J.F. Okulicz, R.S. Shah, R.A. Schwartz, et al., 'Oculocutaneous Albinism', *Journal of the European Academy of Dermatology and Venereology*, (2003) 17, pp. 251–56.

9. Yuju Yamaguchi et al., 'The Regulation of Human Skin Pigmentation', *Journal of Biological Chemistry*, Vol. 282 No. 38, pp. 27, 557–27, 561.

10. Richard A. Sturm, 'Molecular genetics of human pigmentation diversity', *Human Molecular Genetics*, 18 Review Issue: R-9-R-17 (2009).

11. Gregory S. Barsh, 'What Controls Variation in Human Skin Color?', *PLOS Biology* 1(3): e91, 22 December 2003.

12. John J. Abel, 'Experimental and Chemical Studies of the Blood with an Appeal for More Extended Chemical Training for the Biological and Medical Investigator', *Science*, (6 August 1915), 42, 176.

13. M. Kaposi, *Pathology and treatment of diseases of the skin for practitioners and students*, translation of the last German edition under the supervision of James C. Johnston, William Wood & Co., 1895, New York, pp. 479–80.

14. Joyce Carol Oates and Meghan O'Rourke, 'Why we write about grief', *New York Times*, 26 February 2011, http://www.nytimes.com/2011/02/27/weekinreview/27grief.html?pagewanted=2&hpw, accessed 17 March 2012.

15. Hans Eiberg et al., 'Blue eye color in humans may be caused by a perfectly associated founder mutation in a regulatory element located within the HERC2 gene inhibiting OCA2 expression', *Human Genetics*, Vol. 123, No. 2, pp. 177–87.

16. 'Redheads "could be extinct in 100 years"', *The Daily Mail*, 20 August 2007, Mail Online, http://www.dailymail.co.uk/sciencetech/article-476430/Redheads-extinct-100-years.html, accessed 17 March 2012.

17. Chris Thangam, 'Update: Redheads NOT going extinct', *Digital Journal*, 11 September 2007, http://digitaljournal.com/article/226783, accessed 17 March 2012.

18. Ian J. Jackson, 'Pigmentary Diversity: Identifying the genes causing human diversity', *European Journal of Human Genetics*, (2006) 14, pp. 978–80.

19. Maya Angelou, 'Human Family', *Scholastic Scope*, 52,13 (23 February 2004), 21.

Chapter 8

1. D.H. Lawrence and Freida Lawrence, *The First Lady Chatterley*, The Dial Press Inc., 1944, USA, p. 178.

2. E.D. Stevens, 'The evolution of endothermy', *J. Theor. Biol.* 38:597–611, 1973, 9.

3. Ned Stafford, 'The Changing Nature of Food', *Nature*, 468, S16–S17 (23 December 2010).

4. Ramakrishna J., Weiss M.G., 'Health, illness, and immigration: East Indians in the United States, in cross-cultural medicine—a decade later', Special Issue, *Western Journal of Medicine*, September 1992; 157: 265–70.

5. M.N. Bruné Rossel, 'Adaptive thermoregulation in different species

of animals', 2002 presentation, http://www.gfmer.ch/Presentations_En/Pdf/Thermoregulation.pdf, accessed 17 March 2012.

6. Douglas W. Whitman, 'Function and Evolution of Thermoregulation in the Desert Grasshopper Taeniopoda eques', *Journal of Animal Ecology*, Vol. 57, No. 2 (June 1988), pp. 369–83.

7. K. E. Cooper, 'Some Historical Perspectives on Thermoregulation', *J. Appl. Physiol.*, 92:2002, pp. 1717–24.

8. James Hargrove, 'History of the calorie in nutrition', *J. Nutr.*, Vol. 136, No. 12, 1 December 2006, pp. 2957–61.

9. Edward Arens & H. Zhang, 'The skin's role in human thermoregulation and comfort', University of California, Berkeley: Centre for the Built Environment, 2006, http://escholarship.org/uc/item/3f4599hx, accessed 17 March 2012.

10. Kênia C. Bicegoa, Renata C.H. Barros, 'Physiology of temperature regulation: Comparative aspects', *Comparative Biochemistry and Physiology—Part A: Molecular & Integrative Physiology*, Volume 147, No. 3, July 2007, pp. 616–39.

11. Clarence Collison, 'A closer look: Thermoregulation', *Bee Culture*, 2001, Vol. 139, No. 1, pp. 15–17.

12. Andrea Kurz, 'Physiology of thermoregulation', *Best Practice & Research Clinical Anaesthesiology*, Vol. 22, No. 4, December 2008, pp. 627–44.

13. Lefèvre J. Chaleur, *Animale et Bioénergétique*, Masson, Paris, 1911.

14. Wiley-Blackwell, 'Men perspire, women glow: Men are more efficient at sweating, study finds', *ScienceDaily*, 7 October 2010, http://www.sciencedaily.com /releases/2010/10/101007210546.htm, accessed 17 March 2012.

15. J. Waalen, 'Is older colder or colder older? The association of age with body temperature in 18,630 individuals', *J. Gerontol. A. Biol. Sci. Med. Sci.*, 66(5), May 2011, pp. 487–92.

16. Karen Thomas, 'Thermoregulation in Neonates', *Neonatal Network*, Vol 13. No. 2, 1994, http://www2.kumc.edu/instruction/nursing/nrsg856/articles/ThermoregulationinNeonates.pdf, accessed 17 March 2012.

17. G.Mandl and K. Hastings, 'Energy supply systems in skeletal muscle: Lecture 8, Regulation of muscle contraction and force output', McGill University Faculty of Medicine, http://alexandria.healthlibrary.

ca/documents/notes/bom/unit_2/L-08%20Regulation%20of%20
Muscle%20Contraction%20and%20Force%20Output.xml, accessed
17 March 2011.

18. Body Heat, *Science*, Vol. 319, No. 5862, 25 January 2008, p. 391.

19. 'Kungsbrohuset Green Building in Stockholm', Swedish Environmental
Technology Council, http://swentec.se/en/Start/find_cleantech/
Plants/Kungsbrohuset-Green-building-in-Stockholm/, accessed 17
March 2012.

20. J. Caulfield, 'Body heat', *Builder*, Vol. 34, No. 7, 2011, p. 96.

21. Doreen Gildroy, 'In the Heat, the Body', *The American Poetry Review*,
40, 4 (July/August 2011), p. 24.

CHAPTER 9

1. Aristotle (ca. 350 BC), translated by J.A. Smith, *De Anima* (On the
soul), an Internet resource developed by Christopher D. Green,
York University, Toronto, Ontario, http://psychclassics.yorku.ca/
Aristotle/De-anima/, accessed 17 March 2012.

2. Margaret Jourdain (translator and editor), *Diderot's Early Philosophical
Works*, The Open Court Publishing Company, Chicago and London,
1916, p. 68.

3. Zhang Zixuan, 'Coloring the darkness', *China Daily*, 16 February 2011,
http://usa.chinadaily.com.cn/life/2011-02/16/content_12023942.
htm, accessed 17 March 2012.

4. Lawrence D. Rosenblum, 'Painting by Touch', *Psychology Today*, 17
February 2010, http://www.psychologytoday.com/blog/sensory-
superpowers/201002/painting-touch, accessed 17 March 2012.

5. John Bramblitt (artist), *Style Quotidien,* http://www.stylequotidien.
com/2011/11/artist-john-bramblitt/, accessed 17 March 2012.

6. Johann Gottfried Herder (edited and translated by Jason Gaiger),
'Sculpture: Some Observations on Shape and Form from Pygmalion's
Creative Dream', *Brit. J. Aesthetics*, 46 (1), January 2006, pp. 104–06.

7. 'Bacteria Communicate by Touch, New Research Suggests',
ScienceDaily (1 March 2012), http://www.sciencedaily.com/
releases/2012/03/120301143741.htm, accessed 17 March 2012.

8. E.J. Diner, C.M. Beck, J.S. Webb, D.A. Low, C.S. Hayes, 'Identification
of a target cell permissive factor required for contact-dependent

growth inhibition (CDI)', *Genes & Development*, 26 (5), March 2012, pp. 515–25.

9. W.J.V. Osterhout, 'A Comparison of Permeability in Plant and Animal Cells', *J. Biol. Chem.*, 1918, xxxvi, p. 485.

10. 'Plant hormone in mammalian brain—abscisic acid', *Science News*, 6 April 2012.

11. F. Baluska, 'Plants and animals: convergent evolution in action', F. Balugka (ed.), *Plant-Environment Interactions, Signaling and Communication in Plants*, Springer-Verlag, Berlin and Heidelberg, 2009, p. 285.

12. Janet Braam, 'In touch: plant responses to mechanical stimuli', *New Phytologist*, Vol. 165, Issue 2, February 2005, pp. 373–89.

13. Animal Rights, *Encyclopædia Britannica*, 2007, http://www.britannica.com/EBchecked/topic/25760/animal-rights, accessed 17 March 2012.

14. Charles T. Wolfe, 'Early modern epistemologies of the senses: From the nobility of sight to the materialism of touch', Unit for History and Philosophy of Science, University of Sydney, http://sydney.edu.au/science/hps/early_modern_science/publications_and_preprints/Wolfe_Early_modern_epistemologies.pdf, accessed 17 March 2012.

15. Craig Whippo and Roger Hangarter, 'The "sensational" power of movement in plants: A Darwinian system for studying the evolution of behavior', *Am. J. Bot.*, December 2009, 96 (12), p. 2115–27.

16. Arthur Weissmann, 'Friedrich Sigmund Merkel. Part 1: The Man', *The American Journal of Dermatopathology*, Vol. 4, No. 6, December 1982.

17. Arthur Weissmann, 'Friedrich Sigmund Merkel. Part II: The Cell', *The American Journal of Dermatopathology*, Vol. 4 No. 6, December 1982.

18. Kenneth R. Smith Jr, ,Haarschiebe', *Journal of Investigative Dermatology* 69 (1977), pp. 68–74.

19. Gary W. Gill, 'H&E Staining: Oversight and Insights', *Connection*, 2010, http://www.dako.com/index/knowledgecenter/kc_publications/kc_publications_connection/kc_publications_connection14.htm/28829_2010_conn14_h_e_staining_oversights_insights_gill.pdf, accessed 17 March 2012.

20. Kristin M. Morrison, 'Mammalian Merkel cells are descended from the epidermal lineage', *Dev. Biol.*, 336(1), 1 December 2009, pp. 76–83.

21. C. Toker, 'Trabecular carcinoma of the skin', *Arch. Dermatol.*, 105(1), January 1972, pp. 107–10.

22. G.K. Westling, 'Sensori-motor mechanisms during precision grip in

man', Umeå University Medical Dissertations, New series No. 171, Umeå University, 1986.

23. Francis McGlone and David Reilly, 'The Cutaneous Sensory System', *Neuroscience and Biobehavioral Reviews*, 34 (2010), pp. 148–59.

24. Joseph C. Stevens, 'How skin and object temperature influence touch sensation', *Perception & Psychophysics*, (0031-5117), 32 (3), 1 May 1982, p. 282.

25. Ashley Montagu, *Touching: The Human Significance of the Skin*, Perennial Library, Harper & Row, New York, San Francisco and London, 1971, p. 195.

26. Alberto Acerbi and Dominico Parisi, 'The evolution of pain: Advances in Artificial Life', Proceedings of ECAL 2007, Berlin, Springer, 2007, pp. 816–24.

27. David Morris, 'Congenital Absence of Pain', *Postgraduate Medical Journal*, November 1962, p. 641.

28. Adrienne E. Dubin and Ardem Patapoutian, 'Nociceptors: The sensors of the pain pathway', *J. Clin Invest.*, 120(11), 2010, pp. 3760–72.

29. Nachum Dafny, 'Chapter 6: Pain Principles', Neuroscience Online, Department of Neurobiology and Anatomy, The UT Medical School at Houston, http://neuroscience.uth.tmc.edu/s2/chapter06.html, accessed 17 March 2012.

30. Melissa Nann Burke, 'Out of touch: A rare disorder affects woman's sense of touch, pain', *York Daily Record/Sunday News*, 1 July 2011, http://www.ydr.com/living/ci_15326760, accessed 17 March 2012.

31. J.G. Nicholls et al, 'Specific Modalities and Receptive Fields of Sensory Neurons in CNS of the Leech', *AJP-JN Physiol.*, Vol. 31, No. 5, 1 September 1968, pp. 740–56.

32. Amrit Pal Singh, 'Medicinal leech therapy (Hirudotherapy): A brief overview', *Complementary Therapies in Clinical Practice*, Vol. 16, No. 4, November 2010, pp. 213–15.

33. J. Upshaw O'Leary, 'The medicinal leech: Past and present', *The American Surgeon*, Vol. 66, No. 3, 2000, pp. 313–14.

34. John M. Hyson, 'Leech Therapy: A History', *Journal of the History of Dentistry*, Vol. 53, No. I, March 2005, p. 25.

35. S.G. Browne, 'Some aspects of the history of leprosy: The leprosie of yesterday', *Proceedings of the Royal Society of Medicine*, ISSN 0035-9157, Vol. 68, No. 8, August 1975, pp. 485–93.

36. 'Researchers find how leprosy bacterium selects and attacks nerves', *Science News*, 13 November 2000, http://newswire.rockefeller.edu/2000/11/13/researchers-find-how-leprosy-bacterium-selects-and-attacks-nerves/, accessed 17 March 2012.

CHAPTER 10

1. Emily Singer, 'A Better Artificial Skin', *Technology Review*, MIT, Friday, 12 January 2007.
2. Paul Vitello, 'Dr John F. Burke, Dies at 89; Created Synthetic Skin', *The New York Times*, 5 November 2011.
3. I.V. Yannas (ed. Joseph D. Bronzino), *Artificial Skin and Dermal Equivalents: The Biomedical Engineering Handbook*, 2nd Edition, Boca Raton, USA: CRC Press LLC, 2000.
4. Ming Ying et al, 'Silicon nanomembranes for fingertip electronics', *Nanotechnology*, Vol. 23, No. 34, 31 August 2012.
5. 'Utah researcher helps artist make bulletproof skin', AP foreign news, *The Guardian*, Wednesday, 24 August 2011.
6. 'Researchers Turn Skin Cells Into Stem Cells', *ScienceNOW*, 20 November 2007, http://news.sciencemag.org/sciencenow/2007/11/20-01.html, accessed 17 March 2012.
7. Shinya Yamanaka, 'Induction of Pluripotent Stem Cells from Adult Human Fibroblasts by Defined Factors Cell', Vol. 131, No. 5, 30 November 2007, pp. 861–72.
8. David Van Gend, 'An obituary for human cloning', *AFA Journal*, Vol. 32, No.1, 2011.
9. Oprah Winfrey show interview with Dr Mehmet Oz and Michael J. Fox, 31 March 2009: http://www.oprah.com/health/Dr-Oz-on-the-Medical-Benefits-of-Stem-Cells-Video, accessed 17 March 2012.
10. Biological Clock Controls Activation of Skin Stem Cells, *ScienceDaily*, 10 November 2011, http://www.sciencedaily.com/releases/2011/11/111110092354.htm, accessed 17 March 2012.
11. Iain Hutchison, 'Celebrating skin', *The Lancet*, Vol. 376, No. 9736, 17–23 July 2010, pp. 156–57.
12. 'Organic garments in synthetic skin', http://www.skinbag.net/, accessed 17 March 2012.

Index